SINCE 1973

THE GREATEST STORY EVER!

NEW TESTAMENT

PIONEER TO THE THE ACTION BIBLE

THE PICTURE

Script by Iva Hoth

Illustrations by Andre Le Blanc

THE PICTURE BIBLE NEW TESTAMENT
Published by David C Cook
4050 Lee Vance Drive
Colorado Springs, CO 80918 U.S.A.

Integrity Music Limited, a Division of David C Cook
Brighton, East Sussex BN1 2RE, England

ISBN 978-0-8307-9019-7
eISBN 978-0-8307-9152-1

First edition published by David C Cook in 1990 © David C Cook,
ISBN 978-0-7814-3056-9, adapted from *The Picture Bible*,
© copyright 1978, 1998, 2004 David C Cook, ISBN 978-0-7814-3057-9.

The maps on pages 8 and 128 were developed for Bible-in-Life
Sunday school curriculum, © David C Cook.

First Edition Team: C. Elvan Olmstead, PhD, and Jim Townsend, PhD (Bible editors),
Jeannie Harmon and Cheryl Ogletree (revision editors), Andrea Boven (art director),
Paz Design Group

Second Edition Team: Brock Eastman, Stephanie Bennett, Judy Gillispie, Karen Sherry
Cover Design: Brian Mellema

Printed in China
Second Edition 2025

1 2 3 4 5 6 7 8 9 10

031125

Table of Contents

NEW TESTAMENT STORIES

Jesus' Birth and Childhood

Jesus' Ministry

Jesus' Final Days

AND SO I AM GIVING A NEW COMMANDMENT TO YOU NOW--LOVE EACH OTHER JUST AS MUCH AS I LOVE YOU.

John 13 (page 101)

1ST CHINESE DICTIONARY 2000 B.C. | 1500 B.C. | 1ST OLYMPICS 1000 B.C. | ALEXANDER 500 B.C. | 0 | ROME FALLS 500 A.D. | 1000 A.D. | COLUMBUS 1500 A.D. | TODAY 2000 A.D.

BEFORE RECORDED TIME | THE FUTURE

ABRAHAM | MOSES | DAVID | ELIJAH | ESTHER | JESUS BORN

BIBLE HIGHLIGHTS IN TIME

The Church Is Born

Paul

Life in Bible Times

Acts 9 (page 185)

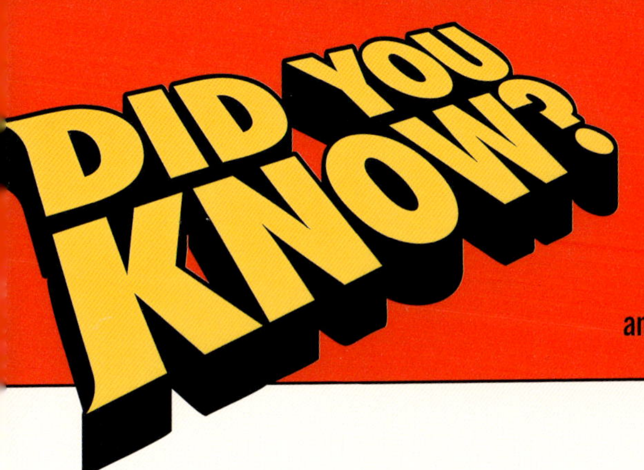

The Bible is filled with many exciting stories. We have provided additional "Did You Know?" fact pages to help you better understand the people and events fooound in God's Word.

STORIES FROM THE

New Testament

New Testament Palestine

The Life of Jesus

From Matthew, Mark, Luke and John

THE WORLD INTO WHICH JESUS CAME

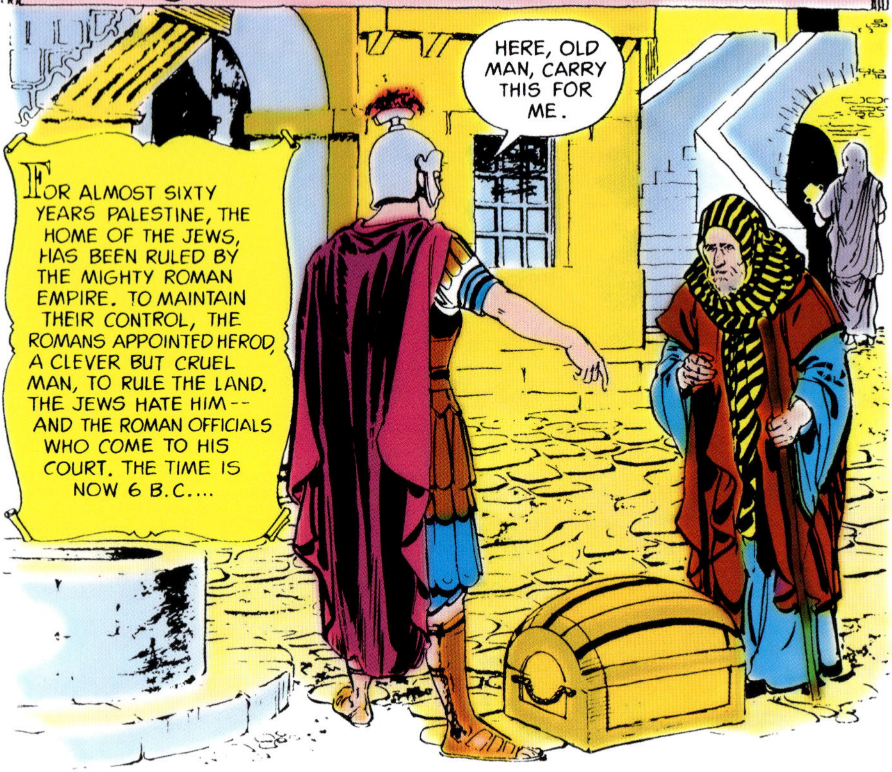

FOR ALMOST SIXTY YEARS PALESTINE, THE HOME OF THE JEWS, HAS BEEN RULED BY THE MIGHTY ROMAN EMPIRE. TO MAINTAIN THEIR CONTROL, THE ROMANS APPOINTED HEROD, A CLEVER BUT CRUEL MAN, TO RULE THE LAND. THE JEWS HATE HIM -- AND THE ROMAN OFFICIALS WHO COME TO HIS COURT. THE TIME IS NOW 6 B.C....

HERE, OLD MAN, CARRY THIS FOR ME.

BUT WHY, MOTHER?
IT'S THE LAW. A ROMAN SOLDIER CAN MAKE A JEW CARRY HIS LUGGAGE FOR A MILE. IT ISN'T RIGHT, BUT THE ROMANS--
THE ROMANS! THEY TAX US FOR EVERYTHING--BUT WE HAVE NO VOICE IN OUR GOVERNMENT. BACK IN THE DAYS OF THE GREAT KING DAVID **WE** WERE THE RULERS!
SHH! SOMEONE MIGHT HEAR YOU.
O GOD, YOU PROMISED TO SEND A DELIVERER. WHEN WILL HE COME?
THE PROPHET MALACHI SAID GOD WOULD FIRST SEND SOMEONE TO PREPARE US FOR THE DELIVERER--AND THAT HELPER HAS NOT YET COME.

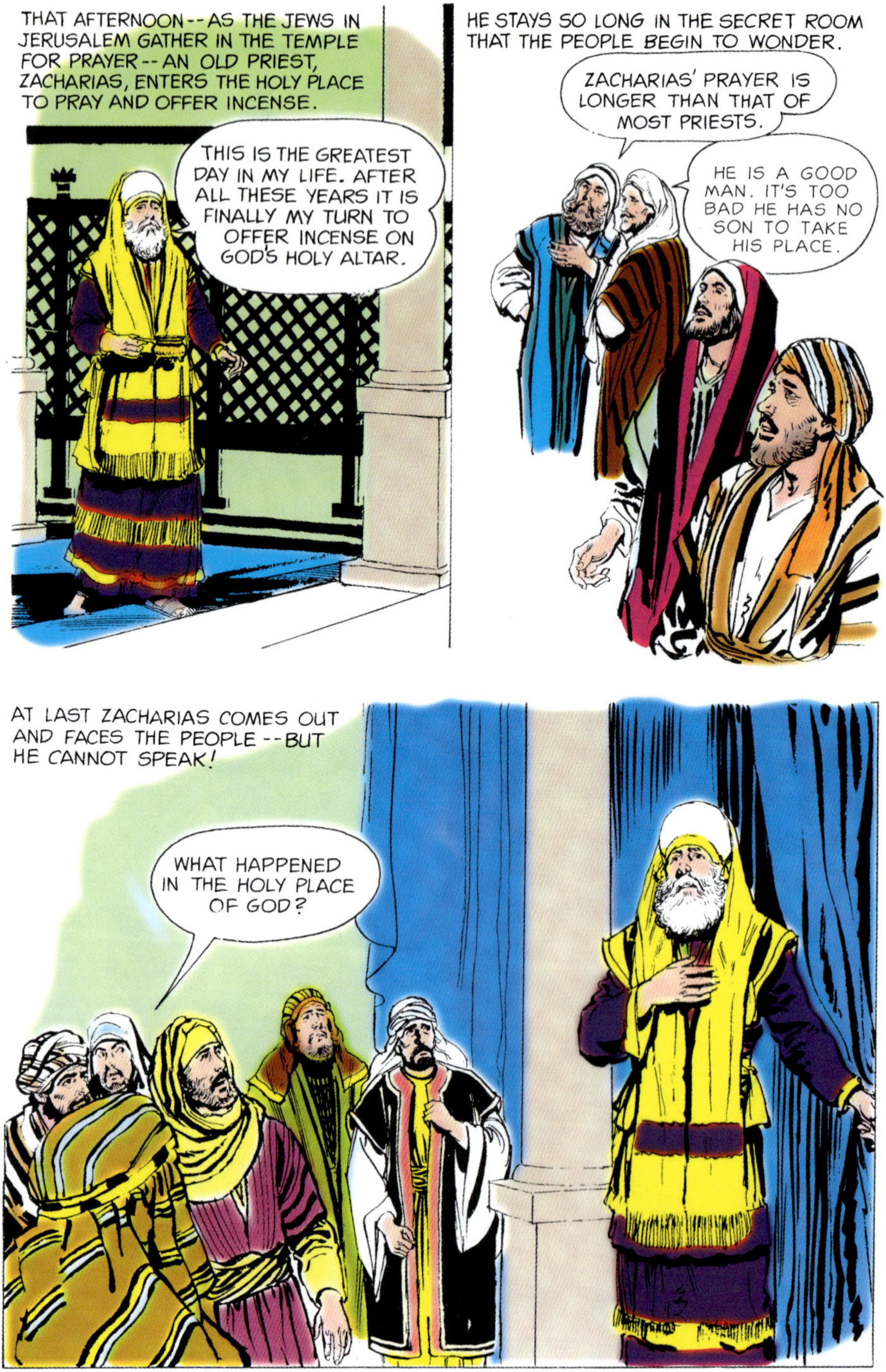

AT LAST ZACHARIAS COMES OUT AND FACES THE PEOPLE -- BUT HE CANNOT SPEAK!

WHAT HAPPENED IN THE HOLY PLACE OF GOD?

A Secret from God

From Luke 1:23-55

ZACHARIAS WRITES A SECOND MESSAGE AND GIVES IT TO HIS WIFE.

OVERJOYED--AND AWED BY THE GREAT TRUST GOD HAS PLACED IN THEM--ZACHARIAS AND ELISABETH PREPARE FOR THE BIRTH OF THEIR SON. IN THE MONTHS THAT PASS THEY OFTEN READ TOGETHER THE PARTS OF SCRIPTURE THAT TELL ABOUT GOD'S PROMISES TO HIS PEOPLE.

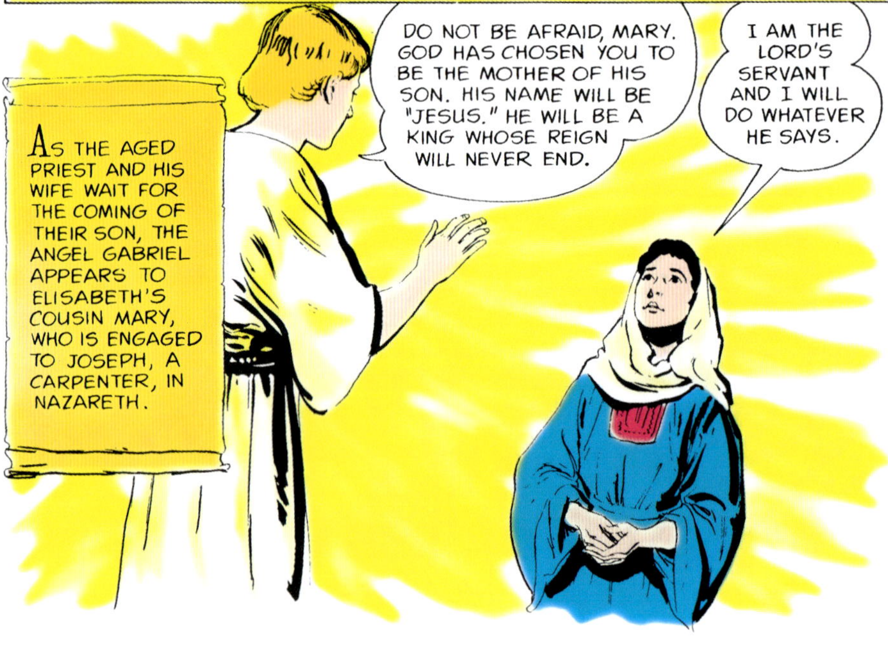

AS THE AGED PRIEST AND HIS WIFE WAIT FOR THE COMING OF THEIR SON, THE ANGEL GABRIEL APPEARS TO ELISABETH'S COUSIN MARY, WHO IS ENGAGED TO JOSEPH, A CARPENTER, IN NAZARETH.

DO NOT BE AFRAID, MARY. GOD HAS CHOSEN YOU TO BE THE MOTHER OF HIS SON. HIS NAME WILL BE "JESUS." HE WILL BE A KING WHOSE REIGN WILL NEVER END.

I AM THE LORD'S SERVANT AND I WILL DO WHATEVER HE SAYS.

MARY TELLS NO ONE OF THE ANGEL'S MESSAGE, BUT IN A FEW DAYS SHE GOES TO THE CARPENTER SHOP TO SEE JOSEPH.
I HAVE DECIDED TO GO AND VISIT MY COUSIN, ELISABETH.
IN JUDAH? I HATE TO HAVE YOU GO ALONE, MARY. IF ONLY THE PERIOD OF OUR ENGAGEMENT WERE OVER AND WE WERE MARRIED. THEN I COULD TAKE YOU THERE.
BUT, MARY LEAVES NAZARETH ALONE.
THE ANGEL SAID THAT ELISABETH IS GOING TO HAVE A SON, TOO. IT WILL BE GOOD TO TALK WITH HER.
AND WHEN SHE REACHES HER COUSIN...
MARY, HOW WONDERFULLY GOD HAS BLESSED YOU! BUT, TELL ME, WHY HAS THE MOTHER OF MY LORD COME TO VISIT ME?
FROM THIS GREETING MARY KNOWS THAT ELISABETH SHARES HER WONDERFUL SECRET. JOYFULLY SHE SINGS ALOUD HER PRAISE TO GOD.
MY SOUL MAGNIFIES THE LORD ... FOR GOD WHO IS MIGHTY HAS DONE GREAT THINGS FOR ME; AND HOLY IS HIS NAME.

A Father's Prophecy

From Luke 1:57-80; 2:1-5

SO THE BABY IS NAMED ACCORDING TO THE INSTRUCTIONS OF THE ANGEL--AND AT THAT MOMENT ZACHARIAS IS ABLE TO SPEAK.
BLESSED BE THE LORD GOD OF ISRAEL; FOR HE HAS VISITED AND REDEEMED HIS PEOPLE ... AND YOU, CHILD, SHALL BE CALLED THE PROPHET OF THE HIGHEST: FOR YOU WILL GO BEFORE THE FACE OF THE LORD TO PREPARE HIS WAYS.
ON THEIR WAY HOME THE PEOPLE TALK ABOUT THE STRANGE EVENTS CONNECTED WITH THE BIRTH OF ZACHARIAS' SON.
THE NAME JOHN --WHAT DOES IT MEAN?
IT MEANS, "GOD HAS BEEN GRACIOUS." GOD MUST HAVE A SPECIAL PURPOSE FOR THAT CHILD.
HOME AGAIN IN NAZARETH, MARY THINKS ABOUT THE PURPOSE GOD HAS FOR HER CHILD. BUT JOSEPH, THE CARPENTER TO WHOM SHE IS ENGAGED, DOES NOT UNDERSTAND WHAT THE ANGEL HAS TOLD MARY ABOUT THE SON THAT IS TO BE BORN. ONE NIGHT AN ANGEL COMES TO HIM.
GOD HAS CHOSEN MARY TO BE THE MOTHER OF HIS SON. YOU MUST CALL THE CHILD JESUS, FOR HE WILL SAVE HIS PEOPLE FROM THEIR SINS.

EARLY THE NEXT MORNING, JOSEPH HURRIES TO SEE MARY.
O MARY, IN A DREAM LAST NIGHT AN ANGEL TOLD ME THAT YOU ARE TO BE THE MOTHER OF THE LORD. I SEE NOW THAT GOD HAS CHOSEN ME TO TAKE CARE OF YOU AND YOUR SON.
SO MARY AND JOSEPH ARE MARRIED, AND MOVE INTO JOSEPH'S HOUSE BESIDE THE CARPENTER SHOP. IN THE EVENINGS WHEN THE DAY'S WORK IS DONE, THEY REST ON THE ROOF TOP--WATCHING THE STARS AND TALKING ABOUT GOD'S PROMISE TO MARY.
BUT ONE DAY JOSEPH COMES HOME FROM THE MARKET PLACE WITH BAD NEWS: CAESAR AUGUSTUS HAS ORDERED EVERYONE TO REGISTER HIS NAME AND PROPERTY. SINCE JOSEPH AND MARY ARE DESCENDANTS OF KING DAVID, JOSEPH MUST GO TO BETHLEHEM, THE CITY OF DAVID.
BUT I CAN'T GO NOW-- AND LEAVE YOU...
YOU MUST GO, JOSEPH, AND I'LL GO WITH YOU. DON'T WORRY-- GOD WILL BE WITH US.
EAGER TO HAVE THE REGISTRATION OVER, THEY SET OUT. SOON OTHERS JOIN THEM ON THE WAY. BUT THE JOURNEY TAKES SEVERAL DAYS, AND AFTER A WHILE JOSEPH AND MARY FALL BEHIND-- UNTIL THEY ARE AMONG THE LAST TO REACH BETHLEHEM.
WE HAVE TRAVELED A LONG WAY AND MY WIFE IS VERY TIRED. I NEED A ROOM.
I'M SORRY, BUT BETHLEHEM IS CROWDED THESE DAYS. THERE'S NO ROOM HERE.

The Night the Angels Sang

From Luke 2:1-15

THAT SAME NIGHT SOME SHEPHERDS ARE WATCHING THEIR SHEEP ON THE HILLS OUTSIDE THE CITY. THEY TALK OF THE CROWDS THAT HAVE COME TO BETHLEHEM.
I'VE HEARD THAT CAESAR AUGUSTUS ORDERED THIS REGISTRATION SO THAT HE CAN COLLECT MORE TAXES. WILL WE NEVER BE FREE FROM THESE FOREIGN TYRANTS?
GOD HAS PROMISED US A DELIVERER. AND ALL MY LIFE I HAVE PRAYED THAT I WOULD LIVE TO SEE HIM.
SUDDENLY-- A GREAT LIGHT SHINES AROUND THE SHEPHERDS.
WHAT IS IT?
O GOD, PROTECT US.
FEAR NOT; FOR I BRING YOU GOOD NEWS OF GREAT JOY FOR ALL THE PEOPLE. FOR TO YOU IS BORN IN THE CITY OF DAVID A SAVIOR, WHO IS CHRIST THE LORD. YOU WILL FIND THE BABY LYING IN A MANGER.

THE ANGELS LEAVE -- THE BEAUTIFUL LIGHT DISAPPEARS. ONCE AGAIN IT IS DARK AND STILL ON THE BETHLEHEM HILLS.

THE ANGEL SAID WE WOULD FIND THE SAVIOR IN A MANGER. LET'S GO TO BETHLEHEM AND SEE HIM.

A King Is Born

From Luke 2:7, 16-20; Matthew 2:1-8

IT IS A STRANGE AND HOLY NIGHT. WHILE THE CROWDED CITY OF BETHLEHEM SLEEPS, THE SON OF GOD IS BORN. LOVINGLY, MARY WRAPS HER BABY IN SWADDLING CLOTHES AND LAYS HIM IN A MANGER... AND THERE THE SHEPHERDS FIND HIM.

AN ANGEL TOLD US THAT THE SAVIOR HAS BEEN BORN. MAY WE SEE HIM?

MARY NODS, AND JOSEPH TURNS THE LAMP A LITTLE SO THAT ITS LIGHT FALLS ON THE MANGER. REVERENTLY THE SHEPHERDS LOOK AT THE BABY JESUS.

O GOD, WE THANK YOU FOR SENDING OUR SAVIOR, AND FOR LETTING US SEE HIM.

QUIETLY, THE SHEPHERDS TURN AWAY...

...AND GO BACK TO THEIR FLOCKS, STILL PRAISING GOD FOR WHAT HAS HAPPENED THAT NIGHT. AT THE SAME TIME IN A LAND FAR TO THE EAST, WISE MEN TALK ABOUT A STRANGE THING THEY HAVE JUST SEEN.
THAT NEW STAR-- IT'S BRIGHTER THAN ALL THE REST. IT MUST HAVE A SPECIAL MEANING.
IT IS A SIGN FROM GOD THAT THE GREAT KING OF THE JEWS HAS BEEN BORN.
LET US GO TO JERUSALEM AND FIND THE KING.
AFTER MONTHS OF TRAVEL, THE WISE MEN REACH JERUSALEM.
WE HAVE COME TO WORSHIP THE ONE BORN TO BE KING OF THE JEWS. PLEASE TELL US WHERE WE CAN FIND HIM.
YOU MUST BE MISTAKEN. NO KING HAS BEEN BORN HERE RECENTLY.

WHEN THE WISE MEN INQUIRE AT THE PALACE, KING HEROD-- WHO HAS COMMITTED MORE THAN ONE MURDER TO PROTECT HIS THRONE-- IS FRIGHTENED. HE CALLS FOR THE CHIEF PRIESTS AND SCRIBES.
IS THERE ANYTHING IN THE SACRED BOOKS TELLING ABOUT A BABY WHO WILL BECOME KING OF THE JEWS?
YES, THE SCRIPTURES SAY HE WILL BE BORN IN BETHLEHEM.
SECRETLY HEROD SENDS FOR THE WISE MEN AND ASKS THEM WHEN THEY SAW THE STAR AND HOW LONG IT TOOK THEM TO COME TO JERUSALEM. THEN HE SPEAKS VERY SLYLY.
LOOK FOR THE CHILD IN BETHLEHEM. WHEN YOU FIND HIM, COME BACK AND TELL ME WHERE HE IS SO THAT I MAY WORSHIP HIM, TOO.
AND WHEN I FIND THAT CHILD, I'LL KILL HIM. NO ONE IS GOING TO BE KING OF THE JEWS BUT ME!

Flight in the Night

From Matthew 2:9-14

FOLLOWING HEROD'S INSTRUCTIONS, THE WISE MEN SET OUT FOR BETHLEHEM. AS THEY LEAVE JERUSALEM, THEY AGAIN SEE THE STAR THEY HAD SEEN IN THE EAST. IT LEADS THEM TO BETHLEHEM, AND THERE...

LOOK! THE STAR HAS STOPPED ABOVE THAT HOUSE!

OUR JOURNEY IS FINISHED! SOON WE'LL SEE THE CHILD WHO IS TO BE KING OF THE JEWS!

PEOPLE IN BETHLEHEM ARE SURPRISED TO SEE THE IMPORTANT-LOOKING STRANGERS STOP BEFORE THE HOUSE WHERE JOSEPH AND MARY NOW LIVE. WHEN THE WISE MEN TELL THEIR REASON FOR COMING, THEY ARE INVITED INSIDE. THERE THEY KNEEL BEFORE THE BABY JESUS.

WE HAVE COME A LONG WAY TO WORSHIP THE ROYAL CHILD.

AND TO BRING HIM GIFTS OF GOLD, FRANKINCENSE, AND MYRRH.

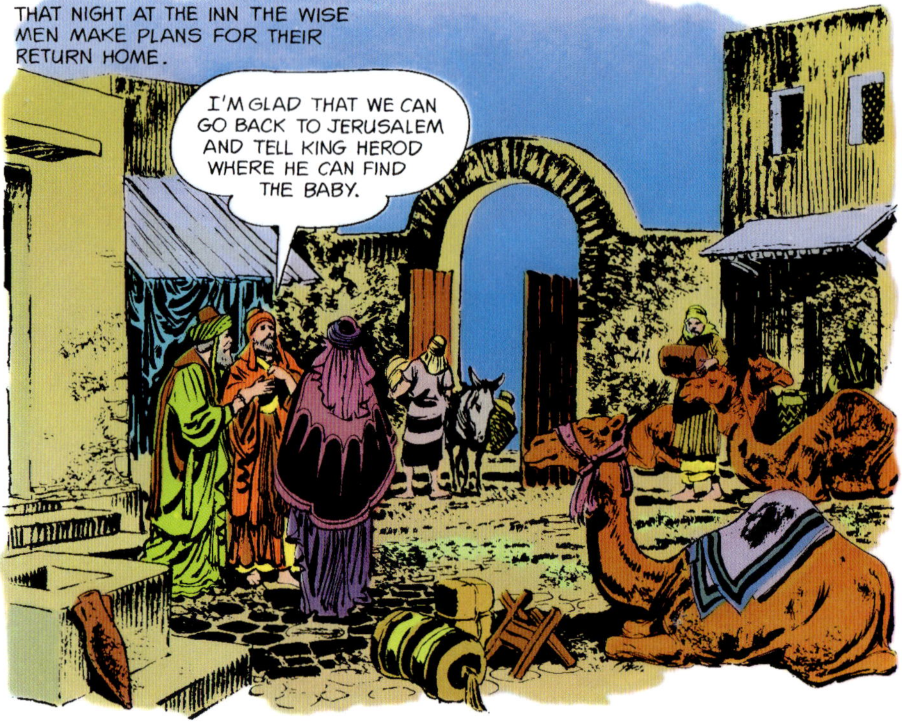

THAT NIGHT AT THE INN THE WISE MEN MAKE PLANS FOR THEIR RETURN HOME.

I'M GLAD THAT WE CAN GO BACK TO JERUSALEM AND TELL KING HEROD WHERE HE CAN FIND THE BABY.

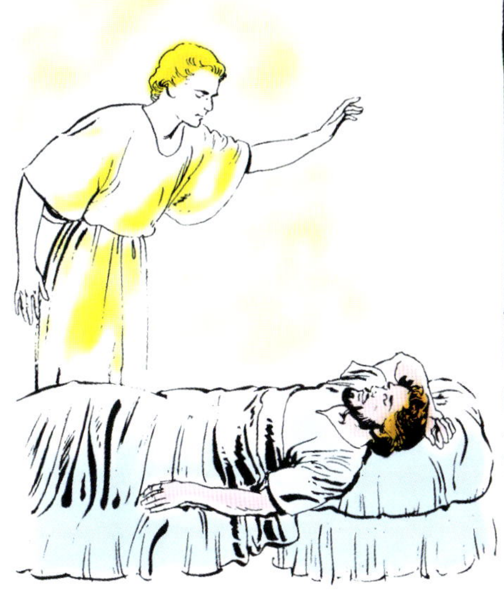
BUT THE WISE MEN ARE NOT THE ONLY ONES WHO ARE WARNED OF HEROD'S ANGER. AN ANGEL OF GOD APPEARS TO JOSEPH, TOO...

MARY! AN ANGEL HAS TOLD ME WE MUST ESCAPE AT ONCE -- TO EGYPT. HEROD WANTS TO KILL JESUS.
KILL JESUS! OH, NO!

IN THE MIDDLE OF THE NIGHT, JOSEPH AND MARY WITH THE BABY JESUS STEAL QUIETLY OUT OF THE CITY.

IN JERUSALEM, HEROD WAITS FOR THE RETURN OF THE WISE MEN. WHEN THEY DO NOT COME, HE SUSPECTS THEY ARE TRYING TO PROTECT THE CHILD -- FROM HIM.
THAT CHILD WILL NEVER LIVE TO TAKE MY THRONE. I'LL KILL EVERY BABY IN BETHLEHEM BEFORE I LET HIM ESCAPE.

Boy in the Temple

From Matthew 2:16-23; Luke 2:40-52

JOSEPH SETS UP HIS CARPENTER SHOP--AND AS THE YEARS PASS, JESUS LEARNS TO HELP HIM. WHEN THE DAY'S WORK IS OVER JESUS LISTENS TO THE ELDERS OF THE TOWN...

IN THE DAYS OF KING DAVID, **WE** WERE THE RULERS.

YES, BUT IN THOSE DAYS PEOPLE OBEYED GOD. TODAY, TOO MANY IGNORE HIS LAWS.

BUT JOSEPH AND MARY OBEY GOD'S COMMANDMENTS, AND TEACH JESUS TO OBEY THEM, TOO. EACH SPRING THEY ATTEND THE PASSOVER FEAST IN JERUSALEM TO THANK GOD FOR DELIVERING THEIR ANCESTORS FROM SLAVERY IN EGYPT. IN THE CARAVAN THAT MAKES THE ANNUAL JOURNEY FROM NAZARETH, THERE IS NO ONE MORE EXCITED THAN JESUS.

THIS YEAR, AS HE WORSHIPS IN THE TEMPLE, JESUS THINKS OF MANY QUESTIONS HE WOULD LIKE TO ASK THE TEACHERS OF THE JEWS.

BUT NO ONE HAS SEEN JESUS. FRANTICALLY, JOSEPH AND MARY TURN BACK TO JERUSALEM. THEY SEARCH THE INNS, THE CROWDED STREETS, AND FINALLY THE TEMPLE.
JESUS! WE HAVE BEEN LOOKING FOR YOU EVERYWHERE.
BUT, MOTHER, DIDN'T YOU KNOW THAT I WOULD BE IN MY FATHER'S HOUSE?
WE ARE SURPRISED AT YOUR SON'S KNOWLEDGE OF THE SCRIPTURES. HIS QUESTIONS SHOW THAT HE HAS THOUGHT A GREAT DEAL ABOUT GOD AND HIS LAWS FOR MAN.
JESUS IS NOT LIKE ANYONE ELSE. EVEN I, HIS MOTHER, DO NOT UNDERSTAND EVERYTHING ABOUT HIM.
JESUS RETURNS WITH JOSEPH AND MARY TO NAZARETH, WHERE HE LIVES UNTIL HE IS 30 YEARS OLD. HE GROWS TALL AND STRONG, AND IS WELL LIKED BY THE PEOPLE OF NAZARETH. GOD IS ALSO PLEASED WITH HIM. SEVENTY MILES AWAY, IN THE WILDERNESS NEAR THE DEAD SEA, A MAN OF THE SAME AGE PREPARES FOR AN ASSIGNMENT THAT WAS PLANNED FOR HIM--EVEN BEFORE HE WAS BORN.

Tempted!

From Luke 3:1–4:4

NEWS SPREADS FAR AND WIDE ABOUT THE MAN WHO LOOKS AND SPEAKS LIKE A PROPHET OF OLD. CROWDS COME OUT FROM JERUSALEM TO HEAR THE MAN CALLED JOHN THE BAPTIST. SOME ARE ONLY CURIOUS, BUT JOHN KNOWS THEIR THOUGHTS.

DO YOU THINK THAT JUST BECAUSE YOU ARE JEWS YOU WILL BE ALLOWED IN GOD'S KINGDOM? NO, YOU MUST REPENT--

THE SCOFFERS TURN AWAY, BUT MANY PEOPLE LISTEN EAGERLY. ONE DAY A CROWD GATHERS AT THE JORDAN RIVER.

ARE YOU THE SAVIOR GOD HAS PROMISED US?

NO. I BAPTIZE WITH WATER, BUT HE WILL BAPTIZE WITH THE HOLY SPIRIT OF GOD. PREPARE YOURSELVES; THE SAVIOR IS COMING!

UNKNOWN TO JOHN, THE VERY ONE HE IS TALKING ABOUT IS IN THE CROWD. JESUS HAS COME DOWN FROM NAZARETH TO HEAR HIM. HE ASKS TO BE BAPTIZED.

WHY DO YOU COME TO **ME** FOR BAPTISM? IT IS **I** WHO NEED TO BE BAPTIZED BY YOU.

JOHN, THIS IS WHAT GOD WOULD WANT US TO DO.

SO JOHN BAPTIZES JESUS. AND WHEN JESUS COMES UP OUT OF THE WATER, THE SPIRIT OF GOD DESCENDS LIKE A DOVE UPON HIM. THEN A VOICE FROM HEAVEN SPEAKS:
THIS IS MY BELOVED SON IN WHOM I AM WELL PLEASED.
THE CROWDS DO NOT UNDERSTAND WHAT HAS HAPPENED--THEY GO HOME, NOT REALIZING THAT THEY HAVE SEEN THEIR SAVIOR. JOHN CONTINUES PREACHING -- REPENT OF YOUR SINS, FOR THE KINGDOM OF GOD IS COMING SOON.
TO JESUS, THE WORDS OF HIS FATHER ARE A SIGN OF APPROVAL, AND THE GIFT OF THE HOLY SPIRIT IS AN ASSURANCE OF HELP FOR THE WORK GOD HAS SENT HIM TO DO. HE GOES INTO THE WILDERNESS -- ALONE -- TO THINK ABOUT HIS PLAN FOR ESTABLISHING GOD'S KINGDOM.
AT THE END OF FORTY DAYS, JESUS IS HUNGRY. AS HE THINKS OF FOOD, HE HEARS THE VOICE OF THE DEVIL TEMPTING HIM TO USE HIS DIVINE POWER FOR HIS OWN BENEFIT. "IF YOU ARE REALLY THE SON OF GOD," THE DEVIL SAYS, "TURN THIS STONE INTO BREAD. AFTER ALL, GOD WOULD NOT WANT HIS BELOVED SON TO BE HUNGRY."
SCRIPTURE SAYS, "MAN SHALL NOT LIVE BY BREAD ALONE, BUT BY THE WORD OF GOD."
THE DEVIL DOESN'T GIVE UP EASILY. HE TRIES AGAIN-- AND THIS TIME WITH A MORE POWERFUL TEMPTATION...

Victory in the Wilderness

From Matthew 4:5-11; John 1:35-46

LISTENING TO JESUS IS SUCH A WONDERFUL EXPERIENCE THAT HOURS GO BY BEFORE ANDREW SUDDENLY REMEMBERS...

MY BROTHER! HE CAME DOWN HERE FROM CAPERNAUM WITH ME TO HEAR JOHN THE BAPTIST. I MUST FIND HIM AND BRING HIM TO SEE YOU.

SIMON EAGERLY FOLLOWS ANDREW BACK THROUGH THE WINDING STREETS OF BETHANY.
THIS IS SIMON, MY BROTHER.
YES, YOU ARE SIMON, BUT FROM NOW ON YOU SHALL BE CALLED PETER, BECAUSE YOU WILL BE LIKE A ROCK.
THE NEXT DAY JESUS GOES NORTH TO GALILEE. HE INVITES ANOTHER YOUNG MAN, PHILIP, TO BE HIS DISCIPLE AND GO WITH HIM.

PHILIP ACCEPTS JESUS' INVITATION. LIKE ANDREW, HE WANTS TO SHARE HIS GOOD NEWS, SO HE HURRIES TO TELL A FRIEND.
NATHANAEL--COME WITH ME! I HAVE FOUND THE SAVIOR! HE IS JESUS OF NAZARETH.
NAZARETH? CAN ANYTHING GOOD COME FROM **THAT** TOWN?

IF WHAT YOU SAY IS TRUE, MEN WOULD GIVE UP EVERYTHING THEY HAVE TO FOLLOW HIM.
COME AND SEE FOR YOURSELF!

NATHANAEL SEES JESUS, BUT HE STILL DOESN'T BELIEVE. THEN JESUS SPEAKS...

Six Jars of Water

From John 1:47-51; 2:1-11, 23-25; 3:1-2

WHEN THEY REACH THE TOWN THEY ARE GREETED BY A FRIEND OF JESUS.
PLEASE COME TO MY WEDDING FEAST --YOUR MOTHER WILL BE THERE.
THANK YOU-- WE WOULD LIKE TO SHARE YOUR HAPPINESS.

DURING THE FEAST MARY DISCOVERS SOMETHING THAT WILL EMBARRASS THE GROOM--THERE IS NO MORE WINE. SHE TELLS JESUS, THEN SHE GOES TO THE SERVANTS.
DO WHATEVER HE TELLS YOU.

FILL THESE JARS WITH WATER.
WHY WATER? IT'S WINE WE NEED.
BUT THE SERVANTS SENSE A STRANGE AUTHORITY IN JESUS, AND THEY OBEY HIM.
NOW TAKE SOME TO THE HEADWAITER.
WHY--IT IS WINE! IT'S A MIRACLE!
THIS MAN MUST BE A PROPHET OF GOD--NO ORDINARY MAN COULD DO SUCH A THING!

THE HEADWAITER IS SO SURPRISED WHEN HE TASTES THE WINE THAT HE CALLS THE GROOM AWAY FROM THE FEAST.

SIR, THE BEST WINE IS USUALLY SERVED FIRST. BUT YOU HAVE SAVED THE BEST TO THE LAST.

I'M GLAD IF PEOPLE ARE HAPPY.

WHEN JESUS' DISCIPLES HEAR ABOUT THE MIRACLE, THEY TOO ARE EXCITED. THEY TALK ABOUT IT AS THEY GO DOWN TO JERUSALEM WITH JESUS FOR THE PASSOVER FEAST. THE CITY IS CROWDED WITH PEOPLE WHO HAVE HEARD JOHN THE BAPTIST TELL ABOUT THE COMING OF THE MESSIAH. "HOW WILL WE RECOGNIZE HIM?" THEY ASK.

AS JESUS WALKS THROUGH THE BUSY STREETS, HE HEALS THE LAME AND THE SICK.

BECAUSE OF THESE MIRACLES, PEOPLE BEGIN TO ASK: "IS JESUS THE MESSIAH?" ONE NIGHT, AFTER THE STREETS ARE EMPTY, A JUDGE OF THE JEWISH SUPREME COURT STEALS THROUGH THE STREETS OF JERU-SALEM ON A SECRET MISSION.

The Judge's Problem

From John 3:3—4:6; Mark 6:14-17

YOU WERE BORN ONCE OF EARTHLY PARENTS. BUT YOU MUST BE BORN AGAIN OF GOD'S SPIRIT TO LIVE IN GOD'S KINGDOM.
I DON'T UNDERSTAND.
YOU CAN'T SEE THE WIND, BUT YOU CAN SEE WHAT IT DOES. YOU CANNOT SEE THE SPIRIT OF GOD, BUT YOU CAN TELL BY THE WAY A MAN LIVES IF HE HAS BEEN BORN AGAIN AND HAS THE SPIRIT OF GOD IN HIS HEART. GOD LOVES THE WORLD, AND HE HAS SENT ME TO GIVE THIS NEW LIFE TO ALL WHO BELIEVE IN ME.
NICODEMUS GOES AWAY--STILL PUZZLED, BUT WANTING TO LEARN MORE ABOUT JESUS AND HIS TEACHINGS.
JESUS SEES THAT MANY OF THE PEOPLE IN JERUSALEM ARE NOT READY TO RECEIVE HIM AS THEIR SAVIOR, SO HE LEAVES THE CITY. IN JUDEA HE TELLS THE PEOPLE ABOUT GOD'S KINGDOM AND WHAT THEY MUST DO TO ENTER IT. HERE, THE PEOPLE LISTEN EAGERLY.
THIS TEACHER IS GREATER THAN ALL THE PROPHETS.
NEWS OF JESUS' SUCCESSFUL MINISTRY IN JUDEA REACHES JOHN THE BAPTIST.
I'VE HEARD THAT JESUS IS BECOMING MORE POPULAR EVERY DAY.
THANK GOD, I HAVE FULFILLED MY MISSION OF PREPARING THE WAY FOR HIM. JESUS' INFLUENCE MUST INCREASE, AND MINE DECREASE.

SOMETIME LATER JESUS RECEIVES NEWS ABOUT HIS LOYAL FRIEND.
HEROD HAS PUT JOHN THE BAPTIST IN PRISON FOR TRYING TO START A REVOLUTION.
REVOLUTION? NO-- THE REAL REASON IS THAT JOHN CONDEMNED HEROD FOR MARRYING HIS BROTHER'S WIFE.
SOON AFTER THIS, JESUS DECIDES TO EXTEND HIS MINISTRY INTO ANOTHER AREA. HE SETS OUT FOR GALILEE, NORTH OF SAMARIA.
AS THEY APPROACH A TOWN IN SAMARIA, JESUS SENDS HIS DISCIPLES ON AHEAD TO BUY SOME FOOD.
IT MAY BE QUICKER TO GO TO GALILEE BY WAY OF SAMARIA, BUT I WONDER IF IT'S WISE. SAMARITANS HATE US JEWS.
WHILE JESUS IS RESTING BESIDE THE WELL, A WOMAN COMES UP WITH A JAR FOR WATER.
A JEW! DOESN'T HE KNOW JEWS AREN'T WELCOME IN SAMARIA?

In Enemy Territory

From John 4:6-44; Luke 4:16-28; Mark 1:16-20

WHEN JESUS TELLS HER THAT HE IS THE SAVIOR FROM GOD, SHE BELIEVES HIM AND RUNS BACK TO THE TOWN TO TELL THE WONDERFUL NEWS.

COME! SEE A MAN WHO HAS TOLD ME THINGS ABOUT MY LIFE THAT NO STRANGER COULD KNOW. HE IS THE PROMISED MESSIAH! THE SAVIOR!

WHILE THE WOMAN IS IN THE TOWN, JESUS' DISCIPLES RETURN AND INVITE HIM TO SHARE THE FOOD THEY HAVE BOUGHT.

THANK YOU, BUT NOT NOW-- I HAVE FOOD THAT YOU DON'T KNOW ABOUT.

WHAT DO YOU MEAN?

MY FOOD IS TO DO THE WILL OF HIM WHO SENT ME. LOOK AT THE PEOPLE WHO ARE EAGER TO HEAR WHAT GOD HAS SENT ME TO TELL THEM.

ALTHOUGH THE SAMARITANS HATE JEWS, MANY OF THEM BELIEVE JESUS TO BE THEIR SAVIOR. "STAY," THEY PLEAD, "AND TELL US MORE ABOUT GOD AND HIS KINGDOM." JESUS REMAINS FOR TWO DAYS -- THEN GOES ON TO THE REGION OF GALILEE.

ON THE SABBATH, IN HIS TOWN OF NAZARETH, HE GOES TO THE SYNAGOGUE. THERE HE READS FROM THE BOOK OF ISAIAH WHICH TELLS ABOUT THE COMING OF THE MESSIAH. THEN HE SITS DOWN TO TEACH.
TODAY THIS SCRIPTURE HAS BEEN FULFILLED IN YOUR EARS.

YOU--THE MESSIAH? WHY, YOU'RE JUST THE SON OF A NAZARETH CARPENTER!

NO PROPHET IS ACCEPTED IN HIS OWN COUNTRY. REMEMBER--IN THE DAYS OF ELISHA THERE WERE MANY LEPERS IN ISRAEL, BUT THE PROPHET HEALED ONLY ONE--A FOREIGNER, NAAMAN.

THE THOUGHT THAT GOD WOULD DO MORE FOR FOREIGNERS THAN FOR THEM--HIS CHOSEN PEOPLE--TURNS THE WORSHIPERS INTO AN ANGRY MOB.
DRIVE HIM OUT OF THE CITY!
KILL HIM!

BUT--SUDDENLY--JESUS TURNS AND LOOKS INTO THE FACES OF THE MEN AND WOMEN WHO HAVE KNOWN HIM FOR THIRTY YEARS. THEN HE WALKS--SLOWLY--THROUGH THEIR MIDST... AND, STRANGELY, NOT A PERSON DARES TO TOUCH HIM.
FROM NAZARETH JESUS GOES TO CAPERNAUM ON THE SEA OF GALILEE. THERE HE FINDS THE BROTHERS HE MET NEAR THE JORDAN RIVER.
PETER! ANDREW! COME WITH ME, AND I'LL MAKE YOU FISHERS OF MEN.
THEY LEAVE THEIR NETS AND GO AT ONCE WITH JESUS. FARTHER DOWN THE SHORE JESUS SEES TWO MORE FRIENDS--JAMES AND JOHN.
COME WITH ME AND BE MY DISCIPLES.

Through the Roof

From Mark 2:1-14

JESUS KNOWS WHAT THE PHARISEES ARE THINKING.

BUT SO THAT ALL MAY KNOW THAT I HAVE DIVINE POWER TO DO BOTH, I SAY TO YOU, "ARISE, TAKE UP YOUR BED, AND GO TO YOUR HOME."

JESUS LEAVES THE HOUSE WHERE HE HAS BEEN TEACHING, AND AS HE PASSES BY THE TOLL HOUSE AT THE CITY GATE...

YOU TAX COLLECTORS ARE ALL ROBBERS. I CAN'T PAY THAT MUCH TAX, AND YOU KNOW IT.

YOU'D BETTER PAY IT! REMEMBER – I HAVE THE POWER OF THE WHOLE ROMAN EMPIRE BEHIND ME.

One Man's Answer

From Matthew 9:9-13; 12:9-14

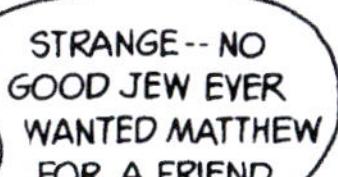

JESUS ANSWERS FOR HIS DISCIPLE.

THE PHARISEES HAVE NO ANSWER TO THIS -- BUT IT MAKES THEM EVEN MORE ANGRY. SO EVERYWHERE JESUS GOES THEY WATCH FOR A CHANCE TO CRITICIZE HIM. ONE SABBATH DAY IN THE SYNAGOGUE...

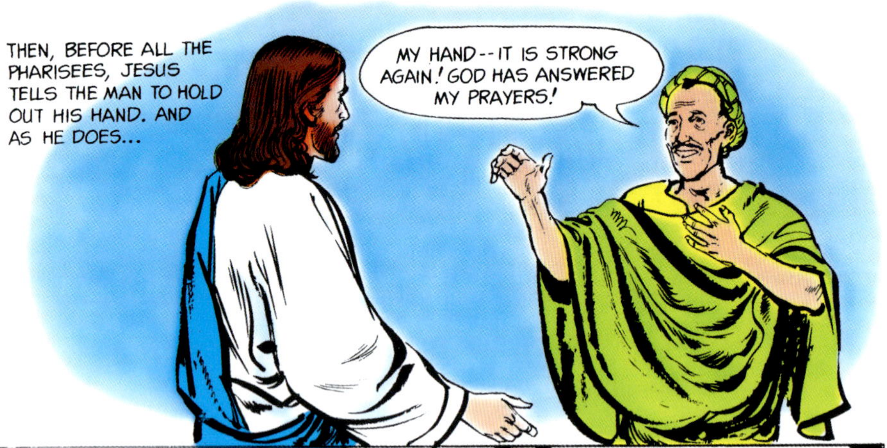

THEN, BEFORE ALL THE PHARISEES, JESUS TELLS THE MAN TO HOLD OUT HIS HAND. AND AS HE DOES...

MY HAND--IT IS STRONG AGAIN! GOD HAS ANSWERED MY PRAYERS!

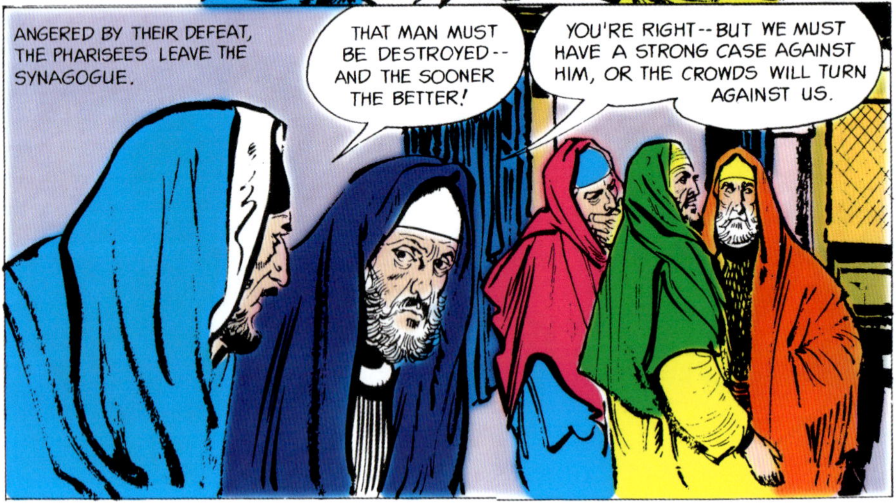

ANGERED BY THEIR DEFEAT, THE PHARISEES LEAVE THE SYNAGOGUE.

THAT MAN MUST BE DESTROYED-- AND THE SOONER THE BETTER!

YOU'RE RIGHT--BUT WE MUST HAVE A STRONG CASE AGAINST HIM, OR THE CROWDS WILL TURN AGAINST US.

Sermon on the Mount

From Luke 6:12-16;
Matthew 5; 6; 7; 8:5-13; 13:45-46;
Mark 4:35-37

JESUS KNOWS THAT THE PHARISEES ARE PLOTTING TO TAKE HIS LIFE, BUT HE DOES NOT LET THIS KEEP HIM FROM CARRYING ON THE WORK GOD SENT HIM TO DO. HE GOES TO A NEARBY MOUNTAIN-- AND SPENDS THE NIGHT IN PRAYER...

...AND FATHER, I THANK THEE FOR GUIDING ME IN THE CHOICES I HAVE MADE THIS NIGHT.

AS THEY COME DOWN THE MOUNTAIN, THEY FIND A LARGE CROWD WAITING FOR JESUS. SO THERE--ON--THE MOUNTAINSIDE JESUS PREACHES A SERMON IN WHICH HE EXPLAINS WHAT MEMBERS OF GOD'S KINGDOM ARE LIKE:

AFTER THE SERMON JESUS TAKES HIS DISCIPLES BACK TO CAPERNAUM. AS THEY ENTER THE CITY THEY ARE STOPPED BY AN OFFICER OF THE ROMAN ARMY.

JESUS! MY SERVANT IS ILL. WILL YOU PLEASE MAKE HIM WELL?

I WILL GO WITH YOU.

I'M NOT WORTHY TO HAVE YOU COME TO MY HOUSE -- BUT I KNOW THAT IF YOU SAY THE WORD MY SERVANT WILL BE HEALED.

NOWHERE IN ALL ISRAEL HAVE I SEEN A MAN WITH SUCH FAITH. GO BACK TO YOUR SERVANT--AND AS YOU BELIEVE, SO IT WILL BE.

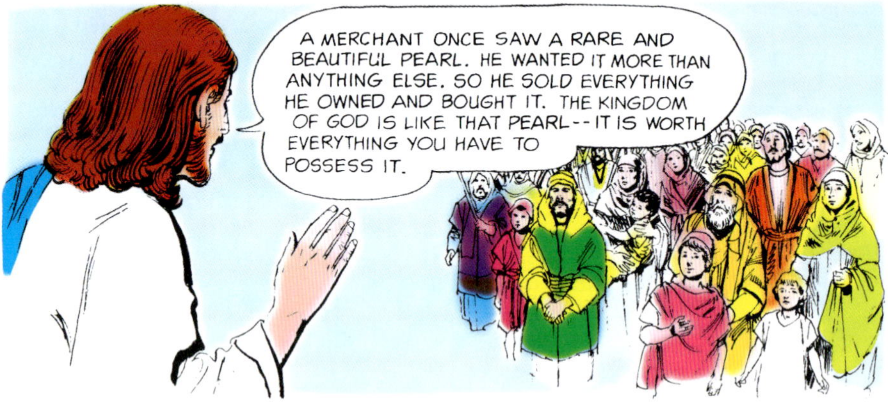

A MERCHANT ONCE SAW A RARE AND BEAUTIFUL PEARL. HE WANTED IT MORE THAN ANYTHING ELSE. SO HE SOLD EVERYTHING HE OWNED AND BOUGHT IT. THE KINGDOM OF GOD IS LIKE THAT PEARL--IT IS WORTH EVERYTHING YOU HAVE TO POSSESS IT.

Mad Man by the Sea

From Mark 4:37-41; 5:1-24, 35

AT THE END OF A DAY OF TEACHING, JESUS ASKS HIS DISCIPLES TO TAKE HIM ACROSS THE SEA OF GALILEE. BUT SOON AFTER HE LIES DOWN TO SLEEP A SUDDEN AND VIOLENT STORM STRIKES.

LOWER THE SAIL!

SECONDS LATER GIANT WAVES ARE POURING OVER THE SHIP.

HELP! WE'RE BEING SWAMPED!

INSTANTLY THE WIND DIES AND THE WAVES VANISH.

IN THE MORNING THE BOAT REACHES SHORE; AND AS JESUS AND HIS DISCIPLES ARE WALKING UP THE BEACH, A MAN POSSESSED BY AN EVIL SPIRIT RUSHES DOWN THE BANK TO MEET JESUS.

AFTER A WHILE JESUS AND HIS DISCIPLES RETURN TO CAPERNAUM. ONCE AGAIN A CROWD GATHERS TO HEAR HIM. BUT JUST AS JESUS BEGINS TO TEACH, JAIRUS, THE CHIEF RULER OF THE SYNAGOGUE, PUSHES HIS WAY THROUGH THE CROWD AND FALLS AT JESUS' FEET.

JESUS GOES WITH JAIRUS -- BUT ON THE WAY THEY ARE MET BY A SERVANT FROM JAIRUS' HOUSEHOLD...

The Mocking Crowd

From Mark 5:38-43; Matthew 9:35—11:1; 14:1-12; John 6:1-10

BUT JAIRUS IS AN IMPORTANT MAN. NEWS ABOUT HIS DAUGHTER SPREADS QUICKLY. AND AS JESUS TRAVELS THROUGH GALILEE, PREACHING AND HEALING, HIS FAME INCREASES. THE PHARISEES WATCH ANGRILY. AS YET THEY HAVE NO REAL CASE AGAINST JESUS AND WITHOUT ONE THEY DARE NOT STIR UP THE EXCITED CROWDS THAT FOLLOW HIM.

NO GREATER PROPHET THAN JOHN EVER LIVED. HE SPENT HIS LIFE DOING THE WILL OF GOD.

SORROWFULLY, JESUS AND HIS DISCIPLES CROSS THE LAKE AND GO UP ON A MOUNTAINSIDE, HOPING TO BE ALONE. BUT A GREAT CROWD FOLLOWS THEM AND JESUS STOPS TO TEACH AND HEAL THE SICK. LATE IN THE AFTERNOON...

PHILIP-- WHERE CAN WE BUY FOOD FOR THESE PEOPLE?

FOR **ALL** OF THEM? WHY, THERE MUST BE 5,000 MEN-- BESIDES THE WOMEN AND CHILDREN.

HERE'S A BOY WITH FIVE LOAVES OF BREAD AND TWO FISHES-- BUT WHAT GOOD IS THAT FOR SUCH A CROWD?

HAVE THE PEOPLE SIT DOWN AND GIVE THE FOOD TO ME.

A miracle is an extraordinary happening—something that couldn't happen without God stepping in to do what no human being could do. It is a way for God to show His power and love for people. Jesus, God's Son, did many miracles while He was on earth.

HERE ARE A FEW OF JESUS' MIRACLES:

- First miracle—Turns water into wine at a wedding reception (p. 37).
- Heals Jairus's daughter (p. 60).
- Walks on water. Disciples think He is a ghost (p. 65).
- Brings a dead man to life (p. 90).
- 153 large fish caught (p. 135).
- Jesus' resurrection is the greatest miracle of all! (p. 129)

Blind man gets his sight (p. 78).

Stormy sea is made calm (p. 57).

There are about 35 miracles recorded in the Gospels. Jesus did many, many more. The Bible says that if all His miracles were written down, the world would not have room for all the books (John 21:25).

Jesus tells many stories called parables during His ministry. A parable is a story that teaches a spiritual lesson by comparing one situation with another. For example, Jesus teaches the disciples about His kingdom by comparing it to types of soil or a treasure in a field. By telling stories, Jesus can explain important truths in a way that people can easily understand.

CHECK OUT THESE STORIES JESUS TELLS:

- Building on Sand Is Risky Business! (Matthew 7:24-27)
- An Expensive Pearl (Matthew 13:45-46)
- One Lamb Is Lost! (Luke 15:3-7)
- Hidden Treasure Found in a Field (Matthew 13:44)
- Widow Woman Who Wouldn't Quit (Luke 18:2-8)
- Mystery of the Lost Coin (Luke 15:8-10)
- Ten Bridesmaids Wait for Groom to Show Up for Wedding (Matthew 25:1-13)

Boy Who Ran Away from Home (p. 87).

Man Attacked on Road to Jericho (p. 82).

No Earthly Throne

From John 6:10-15; Matthew 14:22-30

BUT GOD SENT JESUS TO BE THE SAVIOR, TO BRING PEOPLE INTO THE KINGDOM OF GOD--NOT TO COMMAND ARMIES AND CONQUER THRONES. WHEN JESUS SEES THAT THE CROWD WANTS TO FORCE HIM TO BE A KING, HE QUICKLY CALLS HIS DISCIPLES.

SOON THE STORM HITS...
HOW MUCH FARTHER TO LAND?
WE'RE ONLY HALF WAY.

SUDDENLY THEY LOOK UP TO SEE A FIGURE WALKING ON THE WATER. "A SPIRIT!" THEY CRY IN TERROR. ACROSS THE WAVES A CALM VOICE CALLS OUT: "IT IS I; DON'T BE AFRAID."
LORD! IF IT IS YOU, TELL ME TO COME TO YOU.
COME!

INSTANTLY PETER JUMPS FROM THE BOAT AND STARTS WALKING TOWARD JESUS. BUT WHEN HE SEES THE POWER OF THE WIND, HE LOSES FAITH-- AND BEGINS TO SINK...

Miracle on the Sea

From Matthew 14:30-36; John 6:22-71; Mark 7:1-23; Matthew 16:13-26; 17:1-2

LATER THAT DAY JESUS GOES TO THE SYNAGOGUE IN CAPERNAUM. THE CROWD THAT HE FED THE DAY BEFORE IS THERE ASKING TO BE FED AGAIN. WHEN JESUS PREACHES A SERMON ABOUT THEIR SPIRITUAL NEEDS, MANY OF THEM ARE DISAPPOINTED AND TURN AWAY.

SEEING THIS, THE PHARISEES RESUME THEIR PUBLIC CRITICISM OF JESUS.

WE HAVE SEEN YOUR DISCIPLES EAT WITHOUT WASHING THEIR HANDS. WHY DO YOU LET THEM BREAK OUR LAWS AND DEFILE THEMSELVES?

NOTHING THAT GOES INTO A PERSON'S MOUTH IS DEFILING, BUT THE EVIL WORDS THAT COME OUT DO DEFILE.

SHOCKED BECAUSE HE DEFENDS HIS DISCIPLES, THE PHARISEES TURN AWAY, MORE DETERMINED THAN EVER TO DESTROY JESUS.

KILLED? NEVER!
PETER, YOU DO NOT UNDERSTAND GOD'S PLAN FOR ME. LET ME WARN ALL OF YOU-- IF YOU WANT TO FOLLOW ME, YOU MUST BE PREPARED TO SUFFER AS I WILL SUFFER.
IN SPITE OF WHAT JESUS TELLS THEM, THE DISCIPLES CANNOT BELIEVE THAT HE WILL BE PUT TO DEATH. THEY BELIEVE THAT HE HAS HELPED OTHERS, AND THAT HE WILL HELP HIMSELF. SEVERAL DAYS LATER, JESUS SPEAKS TO PETER, JAMES AND JOHN.
COME WITH ME UP THE MOUNTAIN.
I WONDER WHY...
AFTER A LONG CLIMB TO THE MOUNTAINTOP, JESUS GOES ASIDE TO PRAY. THE DISCIPLES SIT DOWN TO REST, BUT SOON FALL ASLEEP. WHEN THEY AWAKEN THEY SEE SOMETHING STRANGE AND GLORIOUSLY BEAUTIFUL...

A Boy—and His Father's Faith

From Matthew 17:3-23; Mark 9:2-29; Luke 9:28-43

THE NEXT MORNING--ON THE WAY DOWN THE MOUNTAIN--JESUS WARNS HIS DISCIPLES TO TELL NO ONE OF HIS TRANS-FIGURATION UNTIL AFTER HIS RESURRECTION. AFTER WHAT THEY HAVE JUST SEEN THE DISCIPLES CANNOT BELIEVE THAT JESUS WILL DIE--SO THEY ARE PUZZLED WHEN JESUS TALKS ABOUT RISING FROM THE DEAD.

THEY REACH THE VAL-LEY TO FIND A GREAT CROWD GATHERED AROUND THE OTHER DISCIPLES.

THE FATHER OBEYS--BUT THE BOY HAS A SPELL AND FALLS TO THE GROUND AT JESUS' FEET.

WHEN THEY ARE ALONE, THE DISCIPLES TURN TO JESUS.

WHY COULDN'T **WE** HEAL THE BOY?

YOU DID NOT HAVE FAITH. IF YOU HAVE FAITH THE SIZE OF A MUSTARD SEED, NOTHING IS IMPOSSIBLE FOR YOU.

LATER ON THE WAY TO CAPERNAUM, THE DISCIPLES TALK AMONG THEMSELVES ABOUT THE KINGDOM THEY EXPECT JESUS WILL SOON ESTABLISH. ALMOST AT ONCE THEY BEGIN TO QUARREL ABOUT WHICH ONE WILL BE THE GREATEST IN THAT KINGDOM.

Seventy Times Seven

From Matthew 18:1-14, 21-22; John 7:11-52; 8:21-59

AND IF YOU HAVE ANY TROUBLE WITH ANYONE, TALK WITH HIM ABOUT IT AT ONCE. IF HE LISTENS, YOU WILL HAVE WON BACK A FRIEND.
HOW MANY TIMES SHOULD I FORGIVE SOMEONE WHO HAS MISTREATED ME? SEVEN TIMES?
NO, PETER-- SEVENTY TIMES SEVEN. OR AS LONG AS YOU WANT GOD TO FORGIVE YOU.
FROM CAPERNAUM JESUS GOES SOUTH TO PREACH IN JUDEA, AND REACHES JERUSALEM AT THE TIME OF A GREAT RELIGIOUS FEAST. AS HE TEACHES, PEOPLE BEGIN TO WONDER...
IS JESUS THE MESSIAH?
I'VE SEEN HIM DO THINGS THAT NO MAN HAS EVER DONE BEFORE.

ON THE LAST DAY OF THE FEAST THE OFFICERS RETURN TO THE PRIESTS AND PHARISEES.

THE PRIESTS AND PHARISEES ARE FURIOUS-- BUT THEY ARE AFRAID TO FORCE THE ISSUE WHILE THE CITY IS FILLED WITH PEOPLE ATTENDING THE FEAST. BUT THE NEXT DAY...

JESUS RETURNS TO THE TEMPLE TO PREACH. IN THE COURSE OF HIS SERMON HE NOT ONLY POINTS OUT THE SINS OF THE PRIESTS AND PHARISEES BUT DECLARES THAT HE WAS WITH GOD EVEN BEFORE THE DAYS OF THEIR GREAT FOREFATHER, ABRAHAM.

A Beggar Meets Jesus

From John 9:1–10:21; Luke 10:25

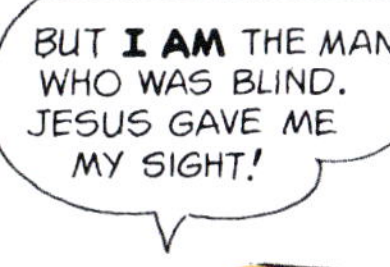
BUT **I AM** THE MAN WHO WAS BLIND. JESUS GAVE ME MY SIGHT!

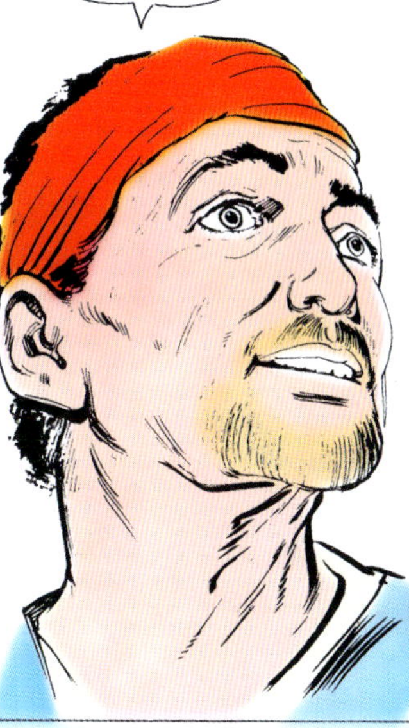

THE NEIGHBORS ARE WORRIED BECAUSE THE MAN HAS BEEN HEALED ON THE SABBATH. THEY TAKE HIM AT ONCE TO THE PHARISEES, WHO INTERPRET THE RULES ABOUT WHAT CAN BE DONE ON THE SABBATH.
THIS JESUS YOU TALK ABOUT IS A SINNER--HE DOESN'T OBEY THE LAWS OF THE SABBATH.
I DO NOT KNOW WHETHER HE IS A SINNER, BUT THIS I DO KNOW: I WAS BLIND AND NOW I SEE.

THE PHARISEES TRY TO MAKE THE MAN TURN AGAINST JESUS, BUT THEY CANNOT, SO THEY PUT HIM OUT OF THE SYNAGOGUE. JESUS LEARNS WHAT HAS HAPPENED, AND SEARCHES FOR THE THE MAN. WHEN HE FINDS HIM THE PHARISEES QUICKLY GATHER AROUND.
DO YOU BELIEVE IN THE SON OF GOD?
WHO IS HE--THAT I MAY BELIEVE IN HIM?

I AM--THE VERY ONE WHO IS SPEAKING TO YOU.
LORD, I BELIEVE!

I AM THE GOOD SHEPHERD; THE GOOD SHEPHERD GIVES HIS LIFE FOR HIS SHEEP. NO ONE CAN TAKE MY LIFE FROM ME, BUT I GIVE IT MYSELF. I HAVE THE POWER TO GIVE IT AND TO TAKE IT AGAIN, FOR I RECEIVED THIS POWER FROM GOD MY FATHER.
THIS MAN IS CRAZY AND IS POSSESSED BY AN EVIL SPIRIT. WHY LISTEN TO HIM?
BUT CAN AN EVIL SPIRIT OPEN THE EYES OF THE BLIND?
THE PHARISEES AND PRIESTS CONTINUE TO ARGUE. SOME THINK THAT JESUS IS WORKING WITH THE DEVIL. OTHERS DECLARE THAT HE IS NOT, BUT THEY REFUSE TO BELIEVE THAT HE IS THE SON OF GOD. A FEW DAYS LATER JESUS AND HIS DISCIPLES LEAVE JERUSALEM FOR A TOUR THROUGH JUDEA.
WHILE JESUS IS PREACHING IN ONE OF THE CITIES A LAWYER IN THE CROWD WAITS FOR A CHANCE TO TEST HIM.
I'LL FIND OUT FOR MYSELF HOW THIS YOUNG TEACHER HANDLES A HARD QUESTION.

Four Travelers to Jericho

From Luke 10:25-40

JESUS REPLIES WITH A STORY WHICH FORCES THE LAWYER AGAIN TO ANSWER HIS OWN QUESTION:

A MAN IS TRAVELING FROM JERUSALEM TO JERICHO. ON THE WAY HE IS ATTACKED BY BANDITS, ROBBED, AND LEFT FOR DEAD.

BY CHANCE A PRIEST COMES BY-- HE SEES THE WOUNDED MAN BUT HE QUICKLY PASSES BY.

A LITTLE LATER A LEVITE, AN ASSISTANT TO THE PRIESTS, COMES ALONG-- BUT HE, TOO, HURRIES BY.

BUT WHEN A SAMARITAN SEES THE INJURED MAN, HE STOPS. ALTHOUGH SAMARITANS ARE BITTER ENEMIES OF THE JEWS, HE BINDS UP THE MAN'S WOUNDS, TAKES HIM TO AN INN, AND PAYS FOR HIS CARE.

WHEN HE FINISHES THE STORY OF THE GOOD SAMARITAN, JESUS ASKS: WHICH ONE OF THE THREE WAS A NEIGHBOR TO THE MAN WHO WAS ROBBED?

THE LAWYER GOES AWAY--AMAZED AT THE SKILL WITH WHICH JESUS ANSWERED HIS QUESTIONS.

NOW I SEE--MY NEIGHBOR IS ANYONE WHO NEEDS ME.

JESUS CONTINUES ON HIS PREACHING TOUR. IN BETHANY HE STOPS TO VISIT HIS FRIENDS: MARY, MARTHA, AND LAZARUS. MARY DROPS EVERYTHING SHE IS DOING TO LISTEN TO JESUS...

The Lord's Prayer

From Luke 10:40–11:2; Matthew 6:9-13; John 10:22-40; Luke 15:1-19

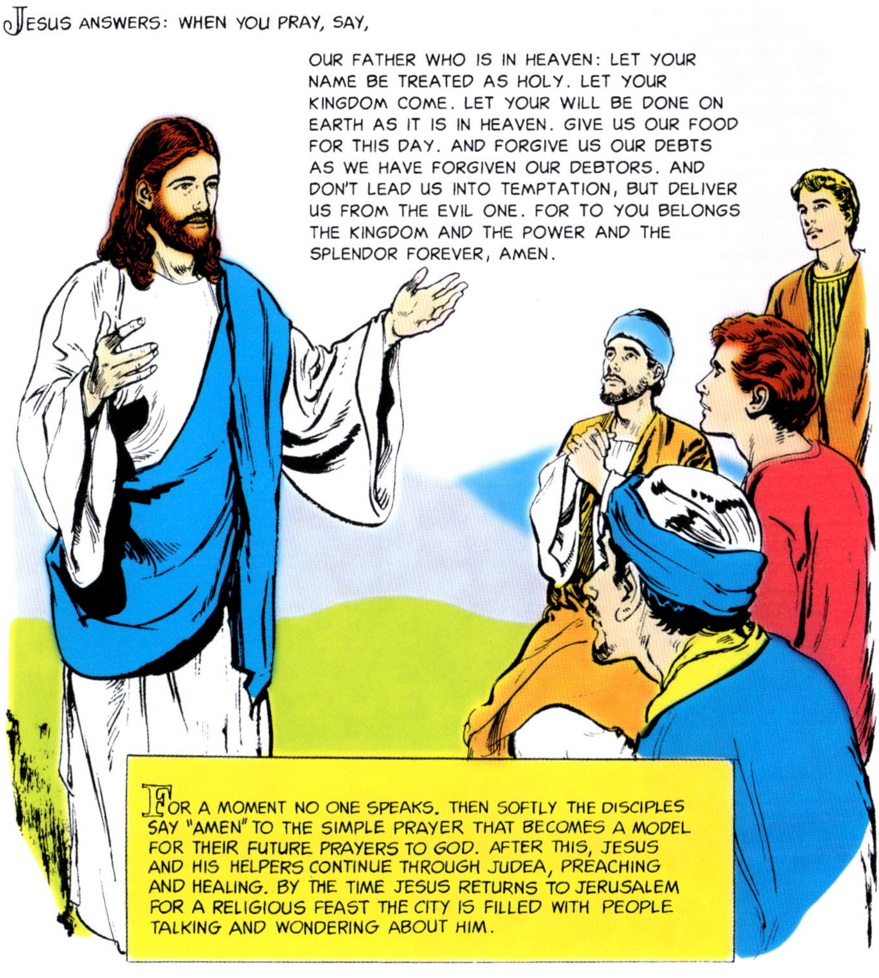

JESUS ANSWERS: WHEN YOU PRAY, SAY,

OUR FATHER WHO IS IN HEAVEN: LET YOUR NAME BE TREATED AS HOLY. LET YOUR KINGDOM COME. LET YOUR WILL BE DONE ON EARTH AS IT IS IN HEAVEN. GIVE US OUR FOOD FOR THIS DAY. AND FORGIVE US OUR DEBTS AS WE HAVE FORGIVEN OUR DEBTORS. AND DON'T LEAD US INTO TEMPTATION, BUT DELIVER US FROM THE EVIL ONE. FOR TO YOU BELONGS THE KINGDOM AND THE POWER AND THE SPLENDOR FOREVER, AMEN.

FOR A MOMENT NO ONE SPEAKS. THEN SOFTLY THE DISCIPLES SAY "AMEN" TO THE SIMPLE PRAYER THAT BECOMES A MODEL FOR THEIR FUTURE PRAYERS TO GOD. AFTER THIS, JESUS AND HIS HELPERS CONTINUE THROUGH JUDEA, PREACHING AND HEALING. BY THE TIME JESUS RETURNS TO JERUSALEM FOR A RELIGIOUS FEAST THE CITY IS FILLED WITH PEOPLE TALKING AND WONDERING ABOUT HIM.

AS JESUS IS WALKING ALONG SOLOMON'S PORCH OF THE TEMPLE, THE PEOPLE SURROUND HIM.

HOW LONG WILL YOU KEEP US WAITING? IF YOU ARE THE MESSIAH, TELL US.

I TOLD YOU, BUT YOU WOULD NOT BELIEVE ME. THE THINGS I HAVE DONE IN MY FATHER'S NAME SHOULD PROVE TO YOU WHO I AM.

DID YOU HEAR THAT? HE CALLED GOD HIS FATHER!

STONE HIM!

JESUS TURNS AND QUIETLY WALKS AWAY, AND--STRANGELY--NO ONE TRIES TO STOP HIM.

JESUS LEAVES JERUSALEM FOR PEREA--WHERE HE CONTINUES TO PREACH AND HEAL THE SICK. AGAIN THE PHARISEES COMPLAIN BECAUSE HE ASSOCIATES WITH SINNERS. JESUS TELLS THEM A STORY...

The Prodigal's Return

From Luke 15:20-32; John 11:1-8

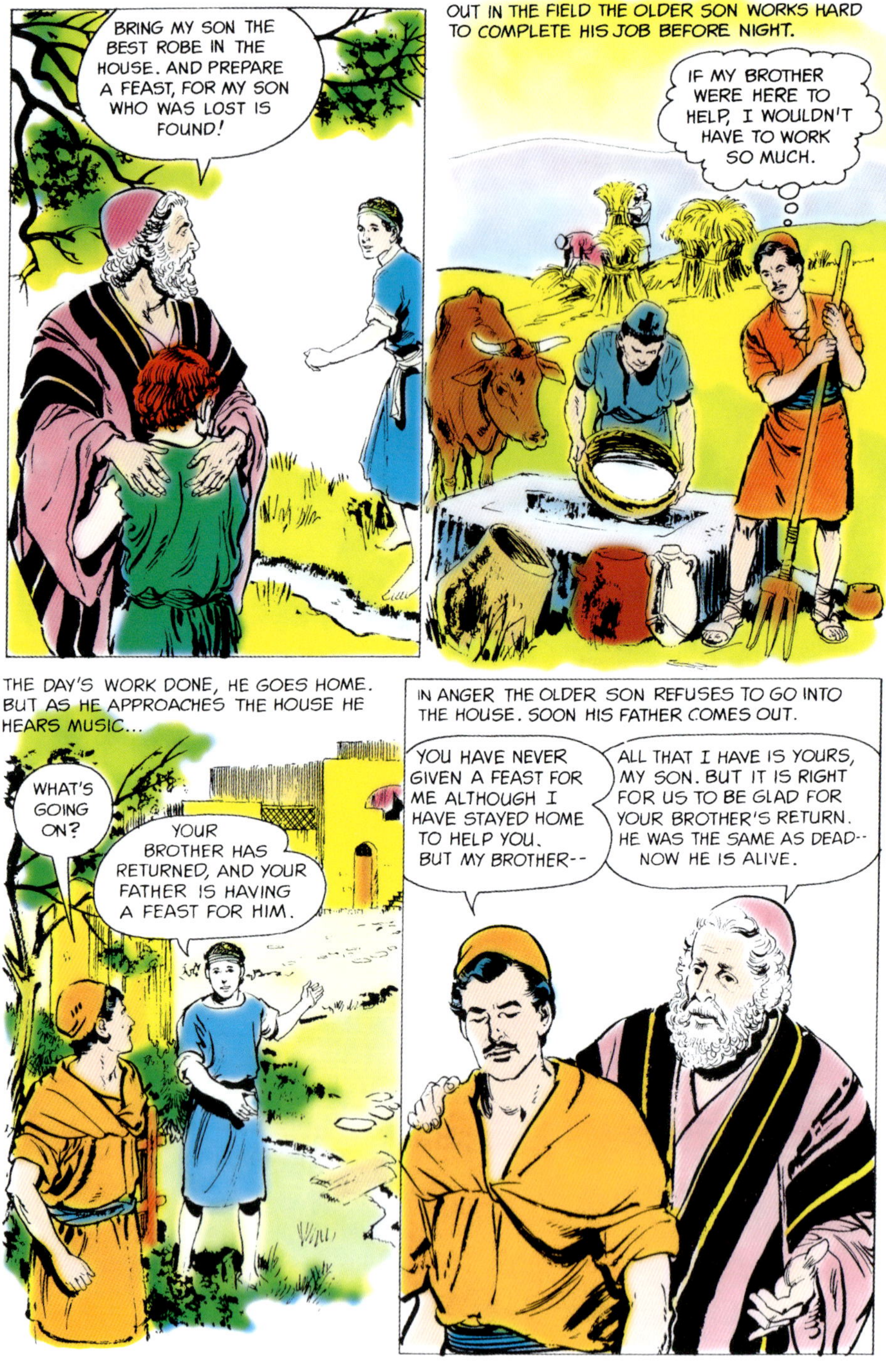

BRING MY SON THE BEST ROBE IN THE HOUSE. AND PREPARE A FEAST, FOR MY SON WHO WAS LOST IS FOUND!

OUT IN THE FIELD THE OLDER SON WORKS HARD TO COMPLETE HIS JOB BEFORE NIGHT.

IF MY BROTHER WERE HERE TO HELP, I WOULDN'T HAVE TO WORK SO MUCH.

THE DAY'S WORK DONE, HE GOES HOME. BUT AS HE APPROACHES THE HOUSE HE HEARS MUSIC...

WHAT'S GOING ON?

YOUR BROTHER HAS RETURNED, AND YOUR FATHER IS HAVING A FEAST FOR HIM.

IN ANGER THE OLDER SON REFUSES TO GO INTO THE HOUSE. SOON HIS FATHER COMES OUT.

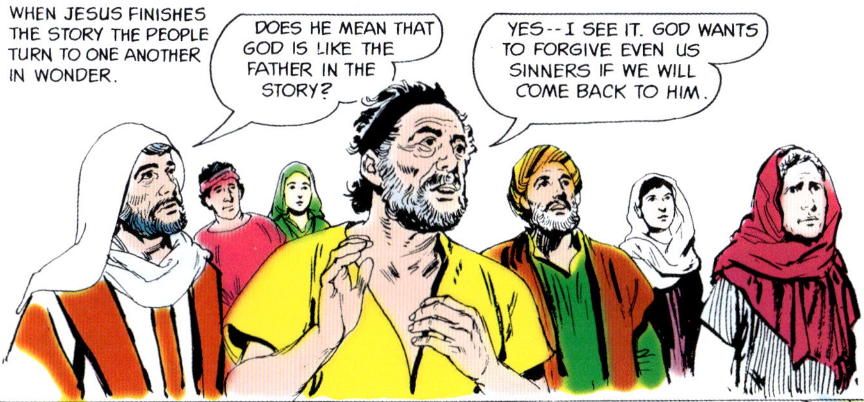

WHEN JESUS FINISHES THE STORY THE PEOPLE TURN TO ONE ANOTHER IN WONDER.

DOES HE MEAN THAT GOD IS LIKE THE FATHER IN THE STORY?

YES--I SEE IT. GOD WANTS TO FORGIVE EVEN US SINNERS IF WE WILL COME BACK TO HIM.

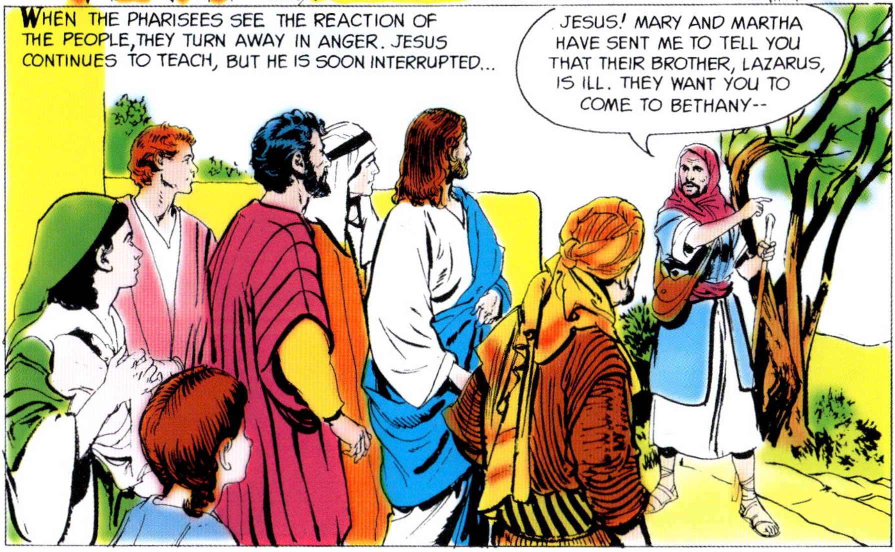

WHEN THE PHARISEES SEE THE REACTION OF THE PEOPLE, THEY TURN AWAY IN ANGER. JESUS CONTINUES TO TEACH, BUT HE IS SOON INTERRUPTED...

JESUS! MARY AND MARTHA HAVE SENT ME TO TELL YOU THAT THEIR BROTHER, LAZARUS, IS ILL. THEY WANT YOU TO COME TO BETHANY--

Called from the Tomb

From John 11:38–54; Luke 18:15–23; 19:1–3

TO THE AMAZEMENT OF THE CROWD, LAZARUS APPEARS!
LAZARUS!
O JESUS, WE THANK YOU!
A MAN RAISED FROM THE DEAD! THE PEOPLE CAN SCARCELY BELIEVE WHAT THEY HAVE SEEN. MANY OF THEM TURN TO JESUS CRYING, "MESSIAH! SON OF GOD!" BUT OTHERS GO INTO JERUSALEM TO TELL THE PHARISEES WHAT JESUS HAS DONE.
IN ANGER AND DESPERATION THE PHARISEES AND CHIEF PRIESTS CALL A MEETING.
IF NEWS OF THIS GETS AROUND THE PEOPLE WILL TRY TO MAKE JESUS A KING.
AND IF THERE'S A REBELLION THE ROMANS WILL BLAME US. WE'LL LOSE OUR POSITIONS AND THE NATION WILL BE DESTROYED.

DON'T YOU SEE? IT IS BETTER TO KILL JESUS THAN TO GET THE WHOLE COUNTRY IN TROUBLE.
CAIAPHAS IS A SHREWD ONE. HE'S FOUND A REASON TO KILL JESUS -- AND HE'LL ALSO FIND A WAY.
WHEN JESUS LEARNS OF THIS NEW PLOT AGAINST HIM, HE GOES OFF TO A QUIET PLACE --TO WAIT UNTIL THE TIME COMES TO FACE HIS ENEMIES.
AS THE TIME FOR THE PASSOVER FEAST APPROACHES, PEOPLE FROM ALL OVER PALESTINE SET OUT FOR JERUSALEM--AND JESUS JOINS THEM.
ON THE WAY THE CROWDS BEG TO SEE AND HEAR JESUS.
NO--NO--TAKE YOUR CHILDREN AWAY. JESUS IS TOO BUSY--
BUT I WANT JESUS TO BLESS MY LITTLE SON.
LET THE LITTLE ONES COME TO ME -- FOR GOD'S KINGDOM IS MADE UP OF PEOPLE WITH LOVE AND TRUST SUCH AS THEIRS.

FARTHER ALONG THE WAY JESUS IS STOPPED BY A YOUNG MAN.
TEACHER, WHAT SHALL I DO TO INHERIT ETERNAL LIFE?
KEEP GOD'S COMMANDMENTS.

BUT I HAVE KEPT THE LAWS --SINCE I WAS A BOY.
YOU NEED TO DO ONE THING MORE --SELL ALL THAT YOU HAVE, GIVE THE MONEY TO THE POOR, AND FOLLOW ME.

THE TRAVELERS CONTINUE ON TOWARD JERUSALEM. BY THE TIME THEY REACH JERICHO, JESUS IS IN THE MIDST OF AN EXCITED, HAPPY THRONG.
PLEASE --LET ME THROUGH!
HO--ZACCHEUS, THE CROOKED LITTLE TAX COLLECTOR, WANTS TO SEE JESUS!

I HAVE TO SEE JESUS--AND I WILL!

Man in the Tree

From Luke 19:4-10; John 12:1-8; Luke 19:29-35

ZACCHEUS, THE WEALTHY TAX COLLECTOR, IS SO SHORT THAT HE CAN'T LOOK OVER THE HEADS OF THE PEOPLE. FRANTICALLY HE RUNS AHEAD OF THE CROWD, CLIMBS A TREE AND WAITS. WHEN JESUS SEES HIM, HE STOPS . . .

ZACCHEUS WONDERS, TOO, BUT HE SOON DISCOVERS THAT BEING IN THE PRESENCE OF JESUS MAKES HIM ASHAMED OF EVERY WRONG THING HE HAS EVER DONE. HE WANTS TO BE FORGIVEN AND START OVER...

FROM JERICHO THE CROWDS CONTINUE THEIR WAY TO JERUSALEM FOR THE GREAT PASSOVER FEAST. THE FESTIVAL IS STILL SIX DAYS AWAY, SO JESUS STOPS IN BETHANY TO VISIT HIS FRIENDS--MARY, MARTHA, AND LAZARUS. AT A SUPPER IN THE HOME OF SIMON THE LEPER, MARY KNEELS BESIDE JESUS AND ANOINTS HIS FEET WITH COSTLY OIL--THEN WIPES THEM WITH HER HAIR.

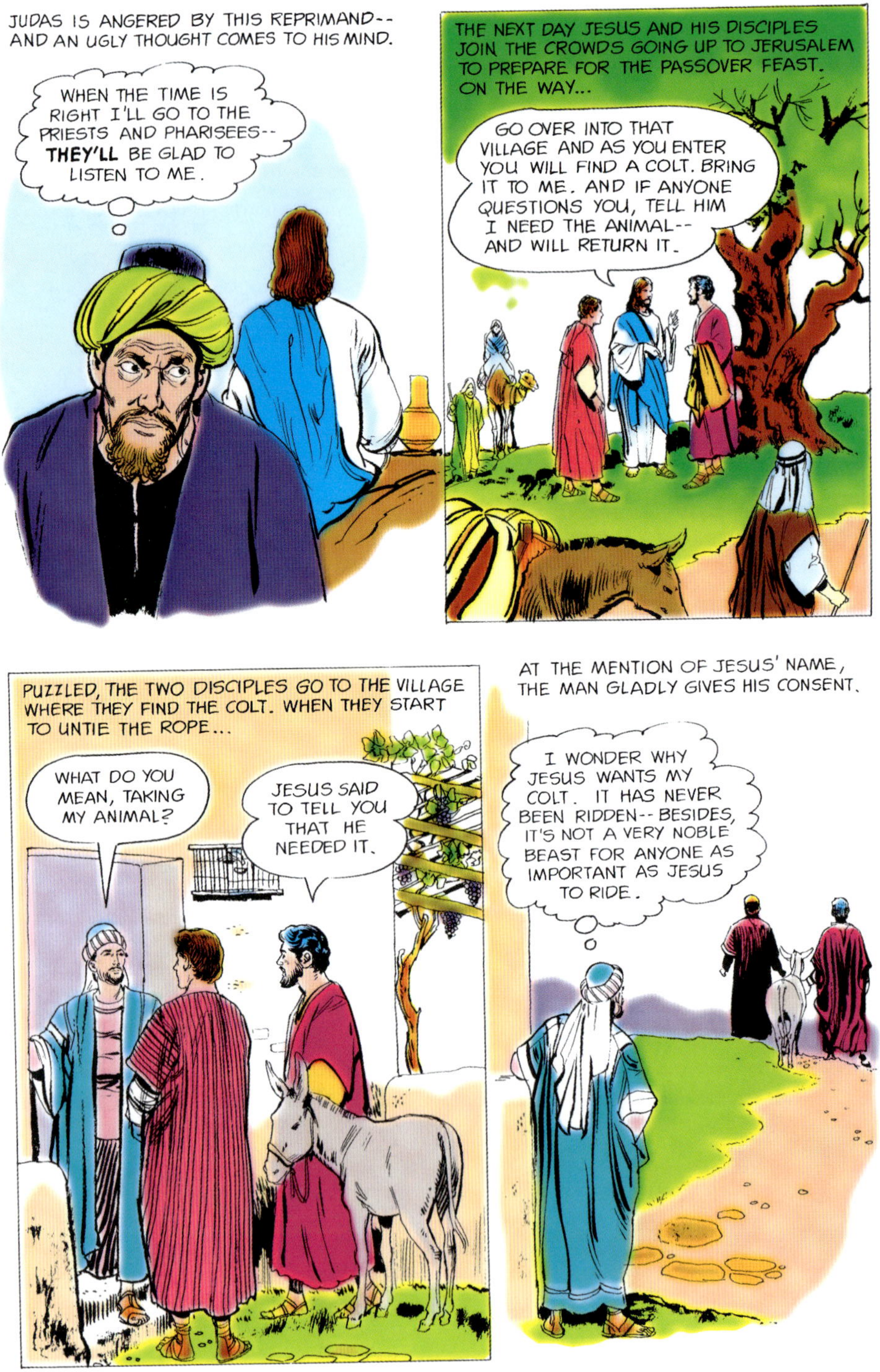

JUDAS IS ANGERED BY THIS REPRIMAND--
AND AN UGLY THOUGHT COMES TO HIS MIND.

WHEN THE TIME IS RIGHT I'LL GO TO THE PRIESTS AND PHARISEES-- **THEY'LL** BE GLAD TO LISTEN TO ME.

THE NEXT DAY JESUS AND HIS DISCIPLES JOIN THE CROWDS GOING UP TO JERUSALEM TO PREPARE FOR THE PASSOVER FEAST. ON THE WAY...

GO OVER INTO THAT VILLAGE AND AS YOU ENTER YOU WILL FIND A COLT. BRING IT TO ME. AND IF ANYONE QUESTIONS YOU, TELL HIM I NEED THE ANIMAL-- AND WILL RETURN IT.

AT THE MENTION OF JESUS' NAME, THE MAN GLADLY GIVES HIS CONSENT.

I WONDER WHY JESUS WANTS MY COLT. IT HAS NEVER BEEN RIDDEN-- BESIDES, IT'S NOT A VERY NOBLE BEAST FOR ANYONE AS IMPORTANT AS JESUS TO RIDE.

Triumphal Entry

From Luke 19:36-38; Matthew 21:10-17; 22:15-17

DURING ITS LONG HISTORY JERUSALEM HAS SEEN MANY PROCESSIONS ENTER ITS GATES--KINGS ON HORSEBACK AND CONQUERORS WITH ARMED LEGIONS--BUT NEVER ONE LIKE THIS.
WHO IS THIS MAN?
JESUS, THE PROPHET OF NAZARETH!
BUT THE NEWS THAT JESUS IS COMING HAS ALREADY SPREAD THROUGH THE CITY. WHEN HE REACHES THE TEMPLE, HE FINDS THE BLIND, LAME, AND SICK THERE WAITING.
RISE UP, MY CHILD, AND WALK.
HOSANNA TO THE SON OF DAVID!

THE CHILDREN'S PRAISE ANGERS THE PRIESTS AND PHARISEES.
DO YOU HEAR WHAT THEY ARE SAYING?
YES, AND HAVE YOU NOT READ IN THE PSALMS THAT OUT OF THE MOUTHS OF CHILDREN GOD BRINGS PERFECT PRAISE?
THAT EVENING JESUS GOES BACK TO BETHANY, BUT ON MONDAY WHEN HE RETURNS TO THE TEMPLE IN JERUSALEM...
I HAVE COME A LONG WAY TO OFFER A SACRIFICE TO GOD, BUT I CAN'T PAY SUCH A HIGH PRICE FOR THE DOVES.
SOMEONE ELSE WILL-- SO MOVE ON.
IN RIGHTEOUS ANGER JESUS DRIVES THE MERCHANTS OUT OF THE TEMPLE.
IS IT NOT WRITTEN IN THE SCRIPTURES THAT "MY HOUSE SHALL BE CALLED A HOUSE OF PRAYER"? BUT YOU HAVE MADE IT A DEN OF THIEVES.

LOOK! **WE** ARE IN CHARGE OF THE TEMPLE, BUT JESUS IS TAKING OVER. I SAY IF WE DON'T GET RID OF HIM **NOW** IT WILL BE TOO LATE.

NO--NO--THERE ARE TOO MANY PEOPLE IN THE CITY WHO BELIEVE IN HIM. WE MUST WAIT FOR THE RIGHT MOMENT.

WHEN JESUS BEGINS TO PREACH, PEOPLE CROWD INTO THE TEMPLE COURTS TO HEAR HIM. BUT BEHIND CLOSED DOORS THE PRIESTS AND PHARISEES PLOT THEIR STRATEGY. BY TUESDAY THEY ARE READY...

MASTER, WE KNOW YOU TEACH THE TRUTH. TELL US, IS IT RIGHT TO PAY TAXES TO CAESAR, OR NOT?

IF HE SAYS "YES," THE PEOPLE WILL TURN AGAINST HIM BECAUSE THEY HATE TO PAY TAXES TO ROME; IF HE SAYS "NO," ROME WILL ARREST HIM FOR TREASON.

HE'S TRAPPED THIS TIME FOR SURE!

The Great Commandment

From Luke 20:23-26; Mark 12:28-34, 38-44; 13; Matthew 26:14-16

QUIETLY JESUS RETURNS THE COIN.

THE PHARISEES ARE ANGRY AT BEING DEFEATED AGAIN, BUT THEY MARVEL AT JESUS' SKILL IN HANDLING THEIR TRICK QUESTION. LATER IN THE DAY ONE OF THEM ASKS ANOTHER DIFFICULT QUESTION.

YOU HAVE SPOKEN THE TRUTH. TO LOVE GOD AND ONE'S NEIGHBOR IS MORE IMPORTANT THAN ALL BURNT OFFERINGS.

YOU ARE NOT FAR FROM THE KINGDOM OF GOD.

THEN JESUS WARNS THE PEOPLE AGAINST THOSE WHO DO GOOD DEEDS JUST TO BE SEEN BY OTHERS. WHEN HE HAS FINISHED SPEAKING HE LOOKS UP TO SEE A PROUD MAN PLACE A LARGE SUM OF MONEY IN THE TEMPLE TREASURY.
THE MAN IS FOLLOWED BY A POOR WIDOW WHO HUMBLY DROPS IN TWO SMALL COINS.
THE WIDOW HAS GIVEN MORE THAN ANYONE ELSE-- FOR SHE HAS GIVEN ALL SHE HAS TO GOD.
WITH THESE WORDS JESUS LEAVES THE TEMPLE -- FOR THE LAST TIME. OUTSIDE JERUSALEM, ON THE QUIET SLOPES OF THE MOUNT OF OLIVES, SOME OF HIS DISCIPLES ASK ABOUT THE FUTURE. JESUS EXPLAINS THAT HIS GOSPEL WILL BE PREACHED THROUGHOUT THE WORLD -- AND THEN HE WILL COME AGAIN TO JUDGE THE WORLD.

JESUS AND HIS DISCIPLES RETURN TO BETHANY. LATER THAT NIGHT JUDAS HURRIES TO JERUSALEM TO CARRY OUT AN IDEA THAT CAME TO HIM WHEN MARY ANOINTED JESUS WITH COSTLY OIL.
I WANT TO SEE THE CHIEF PRIEST.
A MAN NAMED JUDAS ISCARIOT WANTS TO SEE YOU. HE SAYS IT'S URGENT.
JUDAS ISCARIOT? WHY, HE'S ONE OF JESUS' DISCIPLES. SHOW HIM IN.
I KNOW HOW MUCH YOU WANT TO GET RID OF JESUS. WHAT WILL YOU GIVE TO HAVE HIM DELIVERED TO YOU -- AWAY FROM THE CROWDS THAT BELIEVE IN HIM?
THIRTY PIECES OF SILVER.

Secretly—in an Upper Room

From Luke 22:7-13; John 13:1-20, 27-30; Matthew 26:21-25

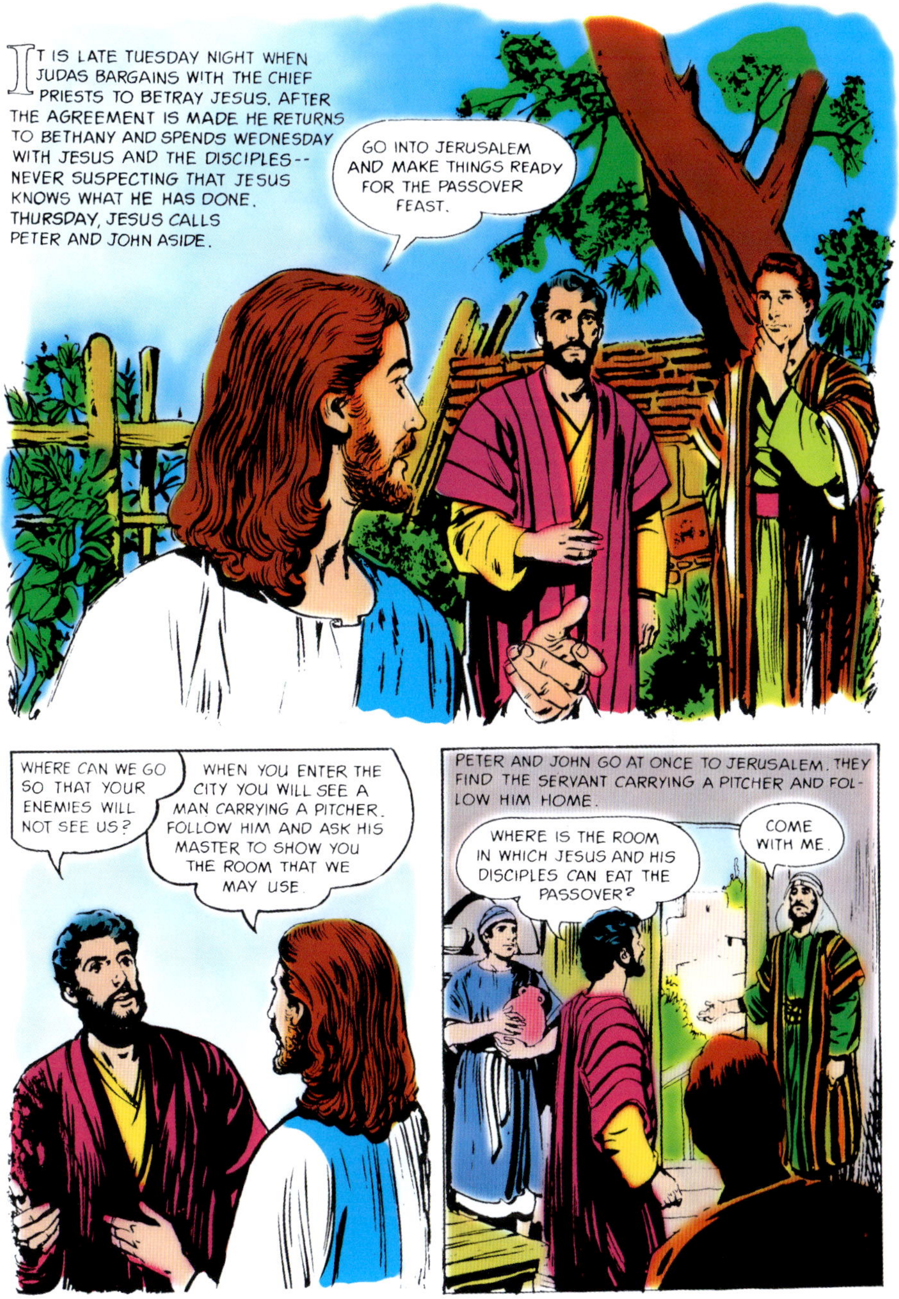

IT IS LATE TUESDAY NIGHT WHEN JUDAS BARGAINS WITH THE CHIEF PRIESTS TO BETRAY JESUS. AFTER THE AGREEMENT IS MADE HE RETURNS TO BETHANY AND SPENDS WEDNESDAY WITH JESUS AND THE DISCIPLES-- NEVER SUSPECTING THAT JESUS KNOWS WHAT HE HAS DONE. THURSDAY, JESUS CALLS PETER AND JOHN ASIDE.

GO INTO JERUSALEM AND MAKE THINGS READY FOR THE PASSOVER FEAST.

THE MAN LEADS THEM QUICKLY UP THE STAIRS TO A BIG UPPER ROOM.

I'M HONORED TO HAVE JESUS CELEBRATE THE PASSOVER IN MY HOUSE.

PETER AND JOHN PREPARE FOR THE FEAST, AND THAT EVENING JESUS JOINS THE TWELVE IN THE UPPER ROOM. AFTER THEY ARE SEATED JESUS KNEELS, LIKE A SERVANT, TO WASH THE FEET OF HIS DISCIPLES.

NO, LORD. I'M NOT GOOD ENOUGH TO HAVE **YOU** WAIT ON ME!

IF YOU DO NOT LET ME SERVE YOU, PETER, YOU WILL HAVE NO PLACE IN MY KINGDOM.

AFTER A FEW MINUTES JESUS MAKES A STARTLING STATEMENT.

AT ONCE THE TRAITOR RISES FROM THE TABLE AND HURRIES AWAY. BUT THE OTHER DISCIPLES DO NOT UNDERSTAND WHY...

The Lord's Supper

From Luke 22:17-20; John 13:33-38; 14; Matthew 26:30, 36-56

IN A LITTLE WHILE I MUST LEAVE YOU. YOU CANNOT FOLLOW ME, BUT BEFORE I GO, LET ME REMIND YOU: LOVE ONE ANOTHER AS I HAVE LOVED YOU.

LORD, WHY CAN'T I FOLLOW YOU? YOU KNOW I'D GIVE MY LIFE FOR YOU.

THE DISCIPLES ARE FRIGHTENED AT THE THOUGHT OF JESUS LEAVING THEM.

QUIETLY, THEY LEAVE THE UPPER ROOM. THEY WALK THROUGH THE MOONLIT STREETS OF THE CITY, OUT AN EAST GATE, AND ACROSS A VALLEY TO THE GARDEN OF GETHSEMANE ON THE MOUNT OF OLIVES.
AT THE ENTRANCE JESUS ASKS EIGHT OF THE DISCIPLES TO WAIT WHILE HE TAKES HIS CLOSEST DISCIPLES, PETER, JAMES, AND JOHN FARTHER INTO THE GARDEN.
THIS IS A SAD NIGHT FOR ME -- STAY HERE AND WATCH WHILE I GO ALONE TO PRAY.
O MY FATHER, IF THOU BE WILLING, REMOVE THIS AGONY FROM ME; NEVERTHELESS, NOT MY WILL, BUT THINE BE DONE.
WHEN JESUS RETURNS TO HIS DISCIPLES, HE FINDS THEM SLEEPING. TWO MORE TIMES HE GOES ASIDE TO PRAY, AND EACH TIME HE FINDS HIS FRIENDS ASLEEP. AFTER WAKING THEM THE THIRD TIME...
ARISE -- THE ONE WHO IS TO BETRAY ME IS NEAR.

AS JESUS SPEAKS, JUDAS LEADS A BAND OF MEN INTO THE GARDEN. ACCORDING TO HIS AGREEMENT, HE IDENTIFIES JESUS WITH A KISS.
GREETINGS, MASTER!
AS THE SOLDIERS TAKE HOLD OF JESUS, PETER DRAWS HIS SWORD. SLASHING WILDLY, HE CUTS OFF THE EAR OF A SERVANT.
PETER, PUT UP YOUR SWORD. DO YOU THINK THAT I CANNOT CALL ON GOD TO SEND LEGIONS OF ANGELS TO PROTECT ME?
QUIETLY JESUS HEALS THE MAN'S EAR. WHEN THE DISCIPLES SEE THAT JESUS IS MAKING NO ATTEMPT TO SAVE HIMSELF, THEY RUN FOR THEIR LIVES. AT AN OFFICER'S COMMAND, THE SOLDIERS BIND JESUS AND TAKE HIM BACK TO JERUSALEM--THE CITY INTO WHICH HE HAD RIDDEN SO TRIUMPHANTLY ONLY A FEW DAYS BEFORE.

Tried and Denied!

From Matthew 26:57-75; John 18:28-38; Luke 23:6-12

WHILE JESUS IS SUFFERING THESE INSULTS, PETER -- WHO HAS SECRETLY FOLLOWED HIM INTO THE CITY--WARMS HIS HANDS BY A FIRE IN THE PALACE COURTYARD. WHILE HE IS TALKING, A MAID STOPS AND LOOKS AT HIM...

YOU WERE ONE OF THOSE WITH JESUS OF NAZARETH.
ME? I DON'T KNOW WHAT YOU'RE TALKING ABOUT.

AFRAID OF BEING QUESTIONED FURTHER, PETER GOES OUT INTO THE HALLWAY, BUT THERE...
THIS FELLOW WAS WITH JESUS.
JESUS? I DON'T EVEN KNOW THE MAN.

ABOUT AN HOUR LATER SOME MEN APPROACH PETER.
DIDN'T I SEE YOU IN THE GARDEN WHEN THE SOLDIERS TOOK JESUS?
YOU ARE A GALILEAN LIKE JESUS. I CAN TELL BY THE WAY YOU TALK.

FOR THE THIRD TIME PETER DENIES KNOWING JESUS-- AND THEN THE COCK CROWS! STARTLED, PETER RAISES HIS HEAD--TO LOOK STRAIGHT INTO THE EYES OF JESUS, WHO IS BEING LED OUT OF THE COURT.
SICK WITH SHAME, PETER RUSHES OUTSIDE, WEEPING BITTERLY.
THREE TIMES I DENIED MY LORD--JUST AS HE SAID I WOULD! O GOD, FORGIVE ME, FORGIVE ME!
IN THE EARLY HOURS OF FRIDAY MORNING THE MEMBERS OF THE JEWISH HIGH COURT, WHICH CANNOT SENTENCE A MAN TO DEATH, TAKE JESUS TO THE ROMAN GOVERNOR, PILATE. CLEVERLY, THEY CHARGE HIM-- NOT WITH BREAKING JEWISH LAWS--BUT WITH TREASON AGAINST ROME. PILATE QUESTIONS JESUS PRIVATELY AND THEN RETURNS HIM TO THE PRIESTS AND CROWDS THAT HAVE GATHERED OUTSIDE.
I DO NOT FIND THIS MAN GUILTY OF ANY CRIME.

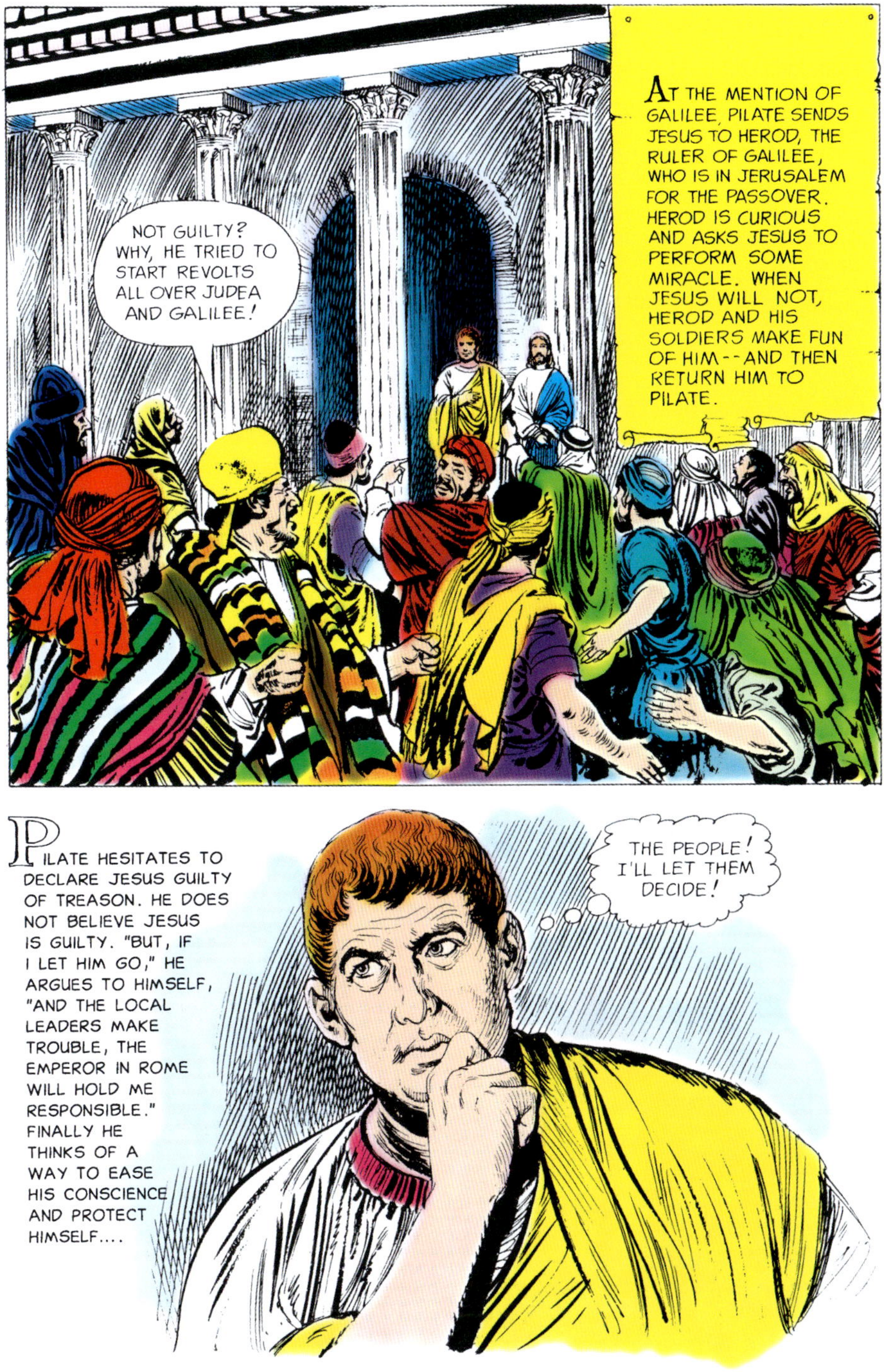

AT THE MENTION OF GALILEE, PILATE SENDS JESUS TO HEROD, THE RULER OF GALILEE, WHO IS IN JERUSALEM FOR THE PASSOVER. HEROD IS CURIOUS AND ASKS JESUS TO PERFORM SOME MIRACLE. WHEN JESUS WILL NOT, HEROD AND HIS SOLDIERS MAKE FUN OF HIM--AND THEN RETURN HIM TO PILATE.

NOT GUILTY? WHY, HE TRIED TO START REVOLTS ALL OVER JUDEA AND GALILEE!

Condemned to Die

From John 18:39—19:16; Matthew 27:3-10

PILATE IS STUNNED. HE MAKES ANOTHER ATTEMPT TO SAVE JESUS.

SCOURGE HIM.

MAYBE THE PEOPLE WILL BE SATISFIED IF THE PRISONER IS PUNISHED.

SO JESUS IS WHIPPED WITH LEATHER THONGS. THEN, IN SPORT, THE SOLDIERS MAKE A CROWN OF THORNS AND PLACE IT ON HIS HEAD.

HAIL, THE KING OF THE JEWS!

HOPING THE SIGHT OF JESUS, BRUTALLY BEATEN, WILL AROUSE THE CROWD'S SYMPATHY, PILATE PRESENTS HIM TO THE MULTITUDE.

BEHOLD THE MAN!

CRUCIFY HIM!

CRUCIFY HIM!

BY THIS TIME PILATE FEELS HIS PREDICAMENT. BUT, NOT WILLING TO ENDANGER HIS POSITION FURTHER, HE SURRENDERS JESUS TO BE CRUCIFIED. AS HE DOES SO, HE WRITES AN INSCRIPTION TO BE PLACED ON JESUS' CROSS.

JESUS OF NAZARETH, THE KING OF THE JEWS.

IT IS PILATE'S WAY OF SHOWING THAT HE HAS NOT BEEN COMPLETELY OUTWITTED

NO! NO! DON'T WRITE THAT HE IS THE KING OF THE JEWS. WRITE THAT HE SAID, "I AM KING OF THE JEWS."

WHAT I HAVE WRITTEN, I HAVE WRITTEN.

TO JESUS, THE HOURS FROM THE TIME HE WAS ARRESTED UNTIL HE IS SENTENCED TO BE CRUCIFIED HAVE BEEN FILLED WITH AGONY.

SOMETIME DURING THOSE DARK HOURS THE TRAITOR, JUDAS, REALIZES WHAT HE HAS DONE AND RUSHES TO THE CHIEF PRIESTS...

I HAVE SINNED-- I HAVE BETRAYED AN INNOCENT MAN.
WHAT IS THAT TO US?
HERE-- TAKE IT. I WANT NO PART OF YOUR DIRTY MONEY.
DRIVEN BY GUILT TOO GREAT TO BEAR, JUDAS GOES OUT AND HANGS HIMSELF.
BUT RETURNING THE MONEY DOES NOT SAVE THE MAN HE HAS BETRAYED. JESUS IS NOW IN THE HANDS OF THE ROMAN SOLDIERS-- WHO PLACE A HEAVY CROSS ON HIS BACK AND FORCE HIM OUT INTO THE STREET THAT LEADS TO A HILL CALLED CALVARY...

A King Is Crucified

From Luke 23:26-46; John 19:25-27

IT IS ABOUT NINE O'CLOCK WHEN JESUS, AND TWO ROBBERS WHO ARE TO BE CRUCIFIED WITH HIM, REACH CALVARY. AND THERE THE SON OF GOD IS NAILED TO A CROSS. ABOVE HIS HEAD IS FASTENED A SIGN: JESUS OF NAZARETH, THE KING OF THE JEWS!

FATHER, FORGIVE THEM: FOR THEY KNOW NOT WHAT THEY DO.

BUT TO THE ROMAN SOLDIERS HE IS ONLY ANOTHER CRIMINAL BEING PUT TO DEATH ACCORDING TO ROMAN LAW.
THIS ROBE IS SEAMLESS -- HOW SHALL WE DIVIDE IT?
IT'S TOO GOOD TO TEAR INTO PIECES. LET'S CAST LOTS FOR IT.
AS JESUS' FRIENDS STAND WATCHING, CURIOUS CROWDS PASS BY. THOSE WHO SCHEMED FOR HIS DEATH TAUNT HIM.
IF YOU'RE THE KING OF ISRAEL, COME DOWN FROM THE CROSS. THEN WE'LL BELIEVE YOU.
IF YOU'RE THE CHRIST, SAVE YOURSELF AND US.

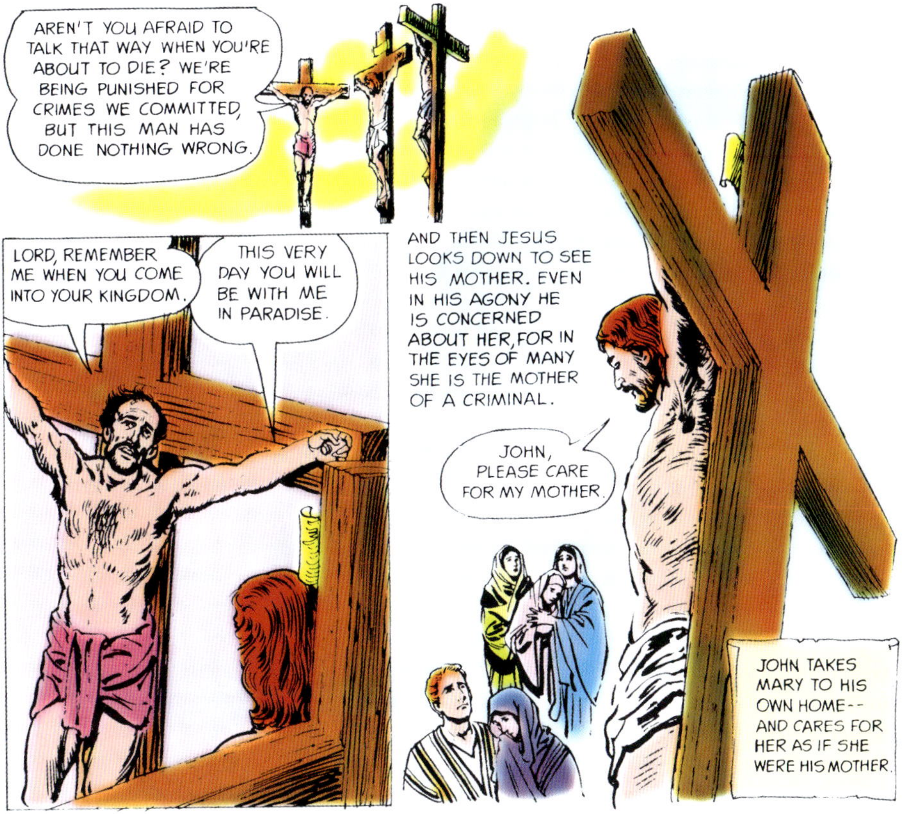

AREN'T YOU AFRAID TO TALK THAT WAY WHEN YOU'RE ABOUT TO DIE? WE'RE BEING PUNISHED FOR CRIMES WE COMMITTED, BUT THIS MAN HAS DONE NOTHING WRONG.

LORD, REMEMBER ME WHEN YOU COME INTO YOUR KINGDOM.

THIS VERY DAY YOU WILL BE WITH ME IN PARADISE.

AND THEN JESUS LOOKS DOWN TO SEE HIS MOTHER. EVEN IN HIS AGONY HE IS CONCERNED ABOUT HER, FOR IN THE EYES OF MANY SHE IS THE MOTHER OF A CRIMINAL.

JOHN, PLEASE CARE FOR MY MOTHER.

JOHN TAKES MARY TO HIS OWN HOME-- AND CARES FOR HER AS IF SHE WERE HIS MOTHER.

IT IS NOW NOON. SLOWLY, A STRANGE SHADOW COVERS THE LAND. FOR THREE HOURS THERE IS DARKNESS, THEN JESUS CRIES OUT TO GOD...

The Sealed Tomb

From Mark 15:38-39; Luke 23:48-49; John 19:38-42; Matthew 27:62-66

OUTSIDE THE CITY, EVEN THE ROMAN OFFICER WHO DIRECTED THE CRUCIFIXION IS AWED BY WHAT HAS HAPPENED. REVERENTLY, HE LOOKS UP AT THE MAN WHO FORGAVE HIS ENEMIES.

TRULY THIS MAN WAS GOD'S SON!

THE PEOPLE, TOO, ARE SHAKEN BY THE EXECUTION. AS THEY TURN BACK TO THE CITY...

I HAD HOPED THAT HE WAS THE ONE WHO WOULD DELIVER US FROM THE ROMANS.

IN JERUSALEM JOSEPH OF ARIMATHEA, A MEMBER OF THE JEWISH HIGH COURT AND SECRETLY A FOLLOWER OF JESUS, GOES BOLDLY TO PILATE.

MAY I HAVE THE BODY OF JESUS SO THAT WE MAY BURY IT BEFORE THE SABBATH?

YES... I'LL GIVE ORDERS TO MY OFFICER IN CHARGE.

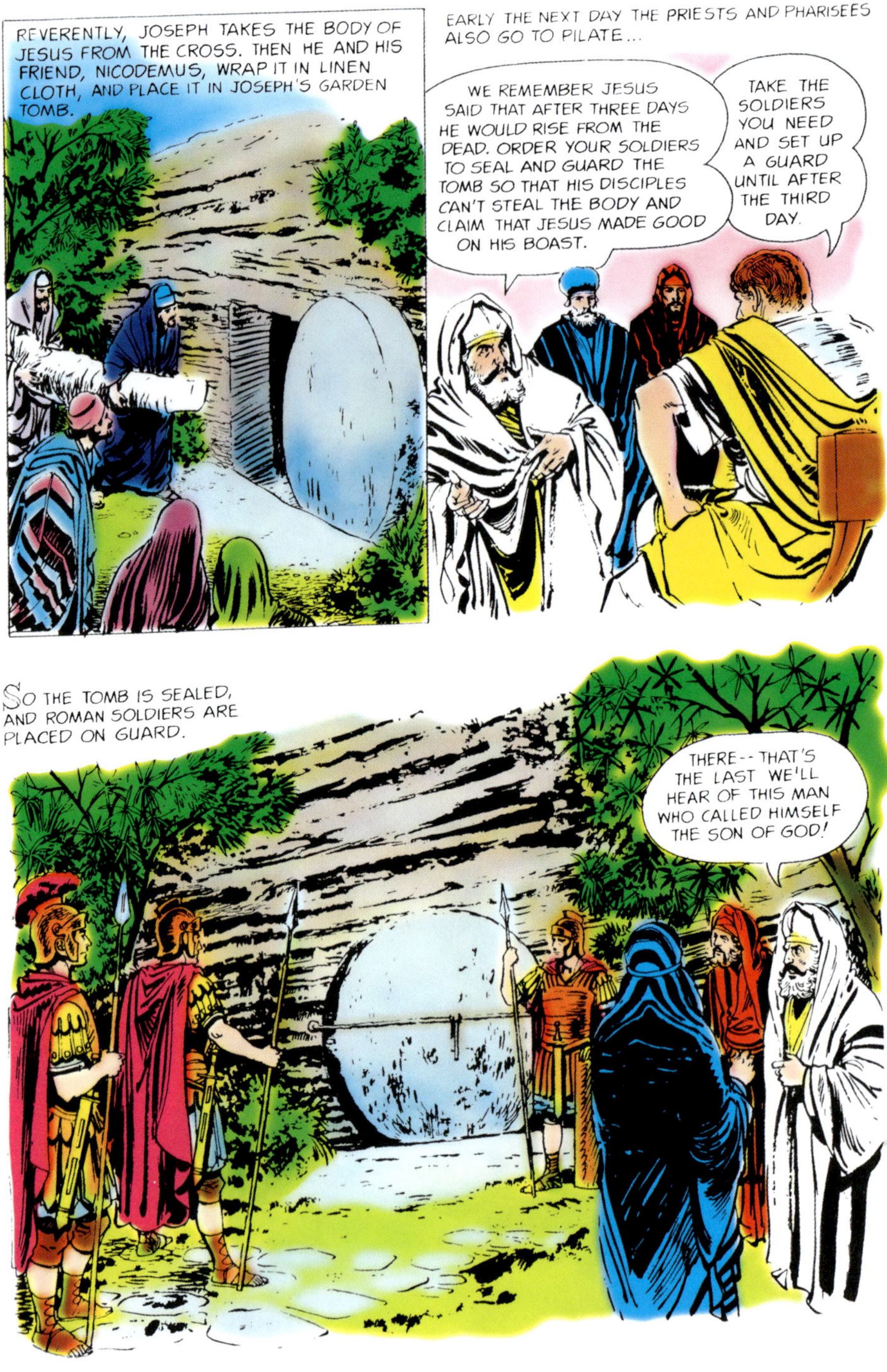

EARLY THE NEXT DAY THE PRIESTS AND PHARISEES ALSO GO TO PILATE...

SO THE TOMB IS SEALED, AND ROMAN SOLDIERS ARE PLACED ON GUARD.

THERE-- THAT'S THE LAST WE'LL HEAR OF THIS MAN WHO CALLED HIMSELF THE SON OF GOD!

When Jesus is arrested, His friends think their hope is gone. In a short time, Jesus is arrested, tried, and crucified. Little do they realize that He will rise a victorious King soon. Here are some of the things that happen.

THIS IS WHAT JESUS EXPERIENCED:

- Judas betrays Jesus for 30 pieces of silver, the price paid for a slave (p. 104).
- When soldiers arrest Jesus, Peter cuts off a guard's ear. Jesus heals the ear immediately (p. 111).
- All of Jesus' friends desert Him when He is arrested (p. 111).

- Soldiers mock Jesus by giving Him a robe, a crown of thorns, and a reed for a scepter (p. 117).

- Jesus is about 33 years old when He dies (Luke 3:23).
- When Jesus dies, an earthquake occurs and the heavy veil in the temple splits in half from top to bottom. This veil is 60 feet long and 30 feet high (p. 124)

Be sure to turn to the other side of this page to see where Jesus went during this time.

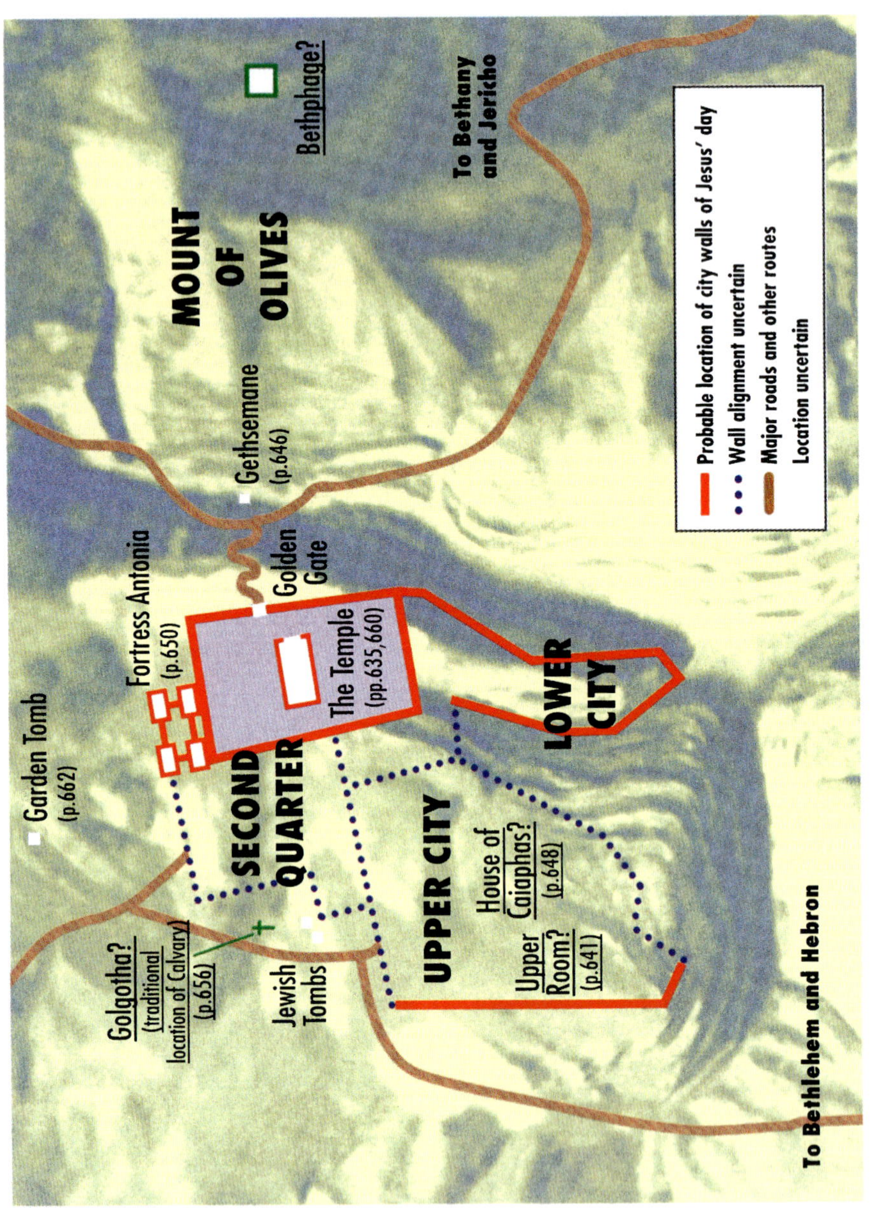

Jerusalem
in the
First Century A.D.

The Lord Is Risen

From Mark 16:1-7; John 20:2-18; Matthew 28:11-15; Luke 24:13-32

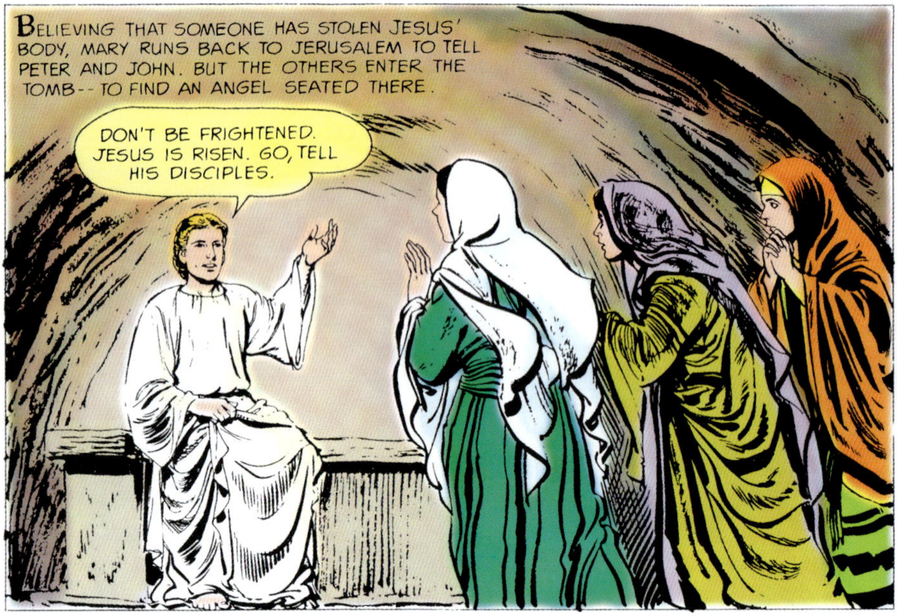

BELIEVING THAT SOMEONE HAS STOLEN JESUS' BODY, MARY RUNS BACK TO JERUSALEM TO TELL PETER AND JOHN. BUT THE OTHERS ENTER THE TOMB-- TO FIND AN ANGEL SEATED THERE.

DON'T BE FRIGHTENED. JESUS IS RISEN. GO, TELL HIS DISCIPLES.

IN THE CITY PETER AND JOHN ARE SO STARTLED BY MARY'S NEWS THAT THEY RACE BACK AHEAD OF HER. WHEN THEY REACH THE TOMB--

BY THE TIME MARY REACHES THE GARDEN THE OTHERS HAVE GONE. IN HER GRIEF SHE DOES NOT RECOGNIZE THE VOICE OF ONE WHO QUESTIONS HER.

SOFTLY JESUS SPEAKS HER NAME--"MARY!" SHE TURNS--AND SEES HER RISEN LORD.

BUT JESUS' FRIENDS ARE NOT THE ONLY ONES WHO ARE EXCITED ABOUT WHAT HAPPENED IN THE GARDEN. IN JERUSALEM THE ROMAN SOLDIERS REPORT TO THE PRIESTS AND PHARISEES. AFRAID OF WHAT MAY HAPPEN IF THE TRUTH IS KNOWN, THEY ACT QUICKLY.

HERE, TAKE THIS MONEY. TELL PEOPLE THAT JESUS' DISCIPLES STOLE HIS BODY.

WHILE THE SOLDIERS SPREAD THEIR LIE, JESUS JOINS TWO OF HIS DISCIPLES ON THE WAY TO EMMAUS. THEY TALK WITH HIM, BUT THEY DO NOT KNOW WHO HE IS.

THAT EVENING AS THEY DINE IN EMMAUS, JESUS BLESSES THE BREAD--AND WHEN HE HANDS IT TO THEM THEY SUDDENLY RECOGNIZE HIM.

Behind Locked Doors

From Luke 24:33-43; John 20:19—21:6

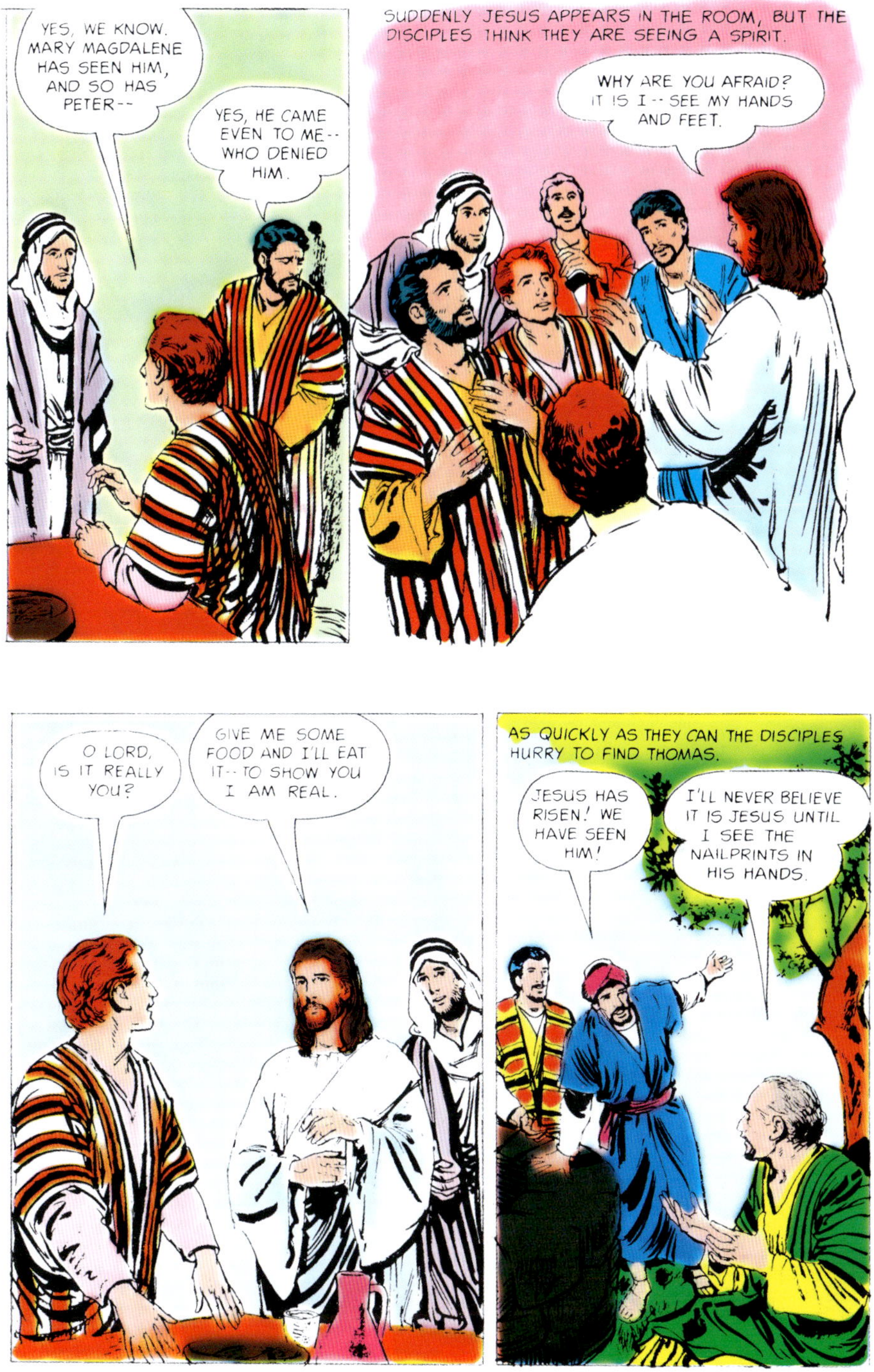

YES, WE KNOW. MARY MAGDALENE HAS SEEN HIM, AND SO HAS PETER--

YES, HE CAME EVEN TO ME--WHO DENIED HIM.

SUDDENLY JESUS APPEARS IN THE ROOM, BUT THE DISCIPLES THINK THEY ARE SEEING A SPIRIT.

WHY ARE YOU AFRAID? IT IS I -- SEE MY HANDS AND FEET.

A WEEK LATER THOMAS IS WITH THE DISCIPLES WHEN THEY MEET AGAIN BEHIND LOCKED DOORS. ONCE MORE JESUS APPEARS TO THEM.
THOMAS, TOUCH MY HANDS AND MY SIDE.

MY LORD AND MY GOD!
BECAUSE YOU HAVE SEEN, THOMAS, YOU BELIEVE. BLESSED ARE THOSE WHO HAVE NOT SEEN AND YET HAVE BELIEVED.
AGAIN JESUS DISAPPEARS FROM THEIR SIGHT.

OBEYING A COMMAND THAT JESUS HAD GIVEN THEM, THE DISCIPLES GO NORTH TO GALILEE. ONE EVENING THEY GO FISHING. THEY FISH ALL NIGHT BUT CATCH NOTHING. AT DAYBREAK THEY SEE THE FIGURE OF A MAN STANDING ON THE SHORE.
CAST YOUR NET ON THE RIGHT SIDE OF THE BOAT.

THEY OBEY—AND SUDDENLY THE NET IS SO FULL OF FISH THEY CANNOT PULL IT IN.

The Last Command

From John 21:7-18; Matthew 28:16-20; Luke 24:44-51

WHEN THEY FINISH EATING, JESUS TURNS TO PETER.
PETER, DO YOU LOVE ME?
YES, LORD, YOU KNOW I DO.
TWICE MORE JESUS ASKS PETER THE SAME QUESTION, AND EACH TIME PETER DECLARES HIS LOYALTY. THEN JESUS GIVES HIM A GREAT ASSIGNMENT.
TAKE CARE OF MY FOLLOWERS, PETER.
A FEW DAYS LATER JESUS APPEARS TO FIVE HUNDRED OF HIS FOLLOWERS, GATHERED AT HIS COMMAND, ON A MOUNTAIN NEAR THE SEA OF GALILEE. HE GIVES THEM A GREAT COMMISSION:
GO YE THEREFORE, AND TEACH ALL NATIONS, BAPTIZING THEM IN THE NAME OF THE FATHER, AND OF THE SON, AND OF THE HOLY SPIRIT, TEACHING THEM TO OBSERVE ALL THINGS WHATSOEVER I HAVE COMMANDED YOU: AND, LO, I AM WITH YOU ALWAYS, EVEN UNTO THE END OF THE WORLD.

DURING THE TIME BETWEEN JESUS' RESURRECTION AND ASCENSION, JESUS MEETS WITH HIS FOLLOWERS AND EXPLAINS HOW--BY HIS DEATH AND RESURRECTION--HE HAS FULFILLED GOD'S MISSION FOR HIM TO BE THE SAVIOR OF THE WORLD. HE CHARGES THEM TO CARRY ON THE WORK. "BUT WAIT IN JERUSALEM," HE ADDS, "UNTIL THE POWER OF GOD'S HOLY SPIRIT COMES UPON YOU."
ON THE FORTIETH DAY AFTER HIS RESURRECTION, JESUS TAKES HIS DISCIPLES TO THE MOUNT OF OLIVES NEAR BETHANY. AND WHILE HE IS BLESSING THEM, HE ASCENDS INTO HEAVEN.

The Acts of the Apostles,

THE FIFTH BOOK OF THE NEW TESTAMENT, TELLS HOW JESUS' DISCIPLES OBEYED HIS COMMAND TO GO INTO ALL THE WORLD AND PREACH THE GOSPEL.

Waiting for a Promise From Acts 1:1-26

THE ANGELS DISAPPEAR, AND PETER TURNS TO THE OTHERS.

LET'S DO WHAT JESUS TOLD US TO DO--GO BACK TO JERUSALEM AND WAIT FOR THE POWER HE PROMISED TO SEND US BEFORE WE BEGIN HIS WORK.

SO THE DISCIPLES, WHO HAD ONCE FLED FOR FEAR OF BEING ARRESTED AS FRIENDS OF JESUS, RETURN TO THE CITY--KNOWING THAT JESUS IS DEPENDING ON THEM TO CARRY ON THE WORK FOR WHICH HE WAS CRUCIFIED.

IN JERUSALEM THEY TAKE LODGING IN AN UPPER ROOM WHICH SOON BECOMES A MEETING PLACE FOR OTHER FOLLOWERS OF JESUS.

JUDAS, WHO BETRAYED OUR LORD, IS DEAD. WE SHOULD APPOINT SOMEONE TO TAKE HIS PLACE.

I NOMINATE BARSABAS.

MATTHIAS.

THE DISCIPLES ASK GOD'S GUIDANCE IN THE CHOICE THEY MAKE-- AND MATTHIAS IS NAMED.
THE LORD HAS BLESSED YOU, MATTHIAS.
FOR THE NEXT TEN DAYS THE DISCIPLES MEET TOGETHER IN PRAYER--WAITING FOR THE COMING OF THE HOLY SPIRIT. AT THE SAME TIME FAITH-FUL JEWS FROM ALL OVER PALESTINE, AND EVEN DISTANT COUNTRIES, CROWD INTO JERUSALEM TO CELEBRATE THE FEAST OF THANKS-GIVING CALLED PENTECOST.

MANY OF THE PILGRIMS PASS BY THE PLACE CALLED CALVARY, AND ARE REMINDED OF JESUS' CRUCIFIXION.
ROMAN SOLDIERS SAY JESUS' DISCIPLES STOLE HIS BODY FROM THE TOMB AND CLAIM HE ROSE FROM THE DEAD AS HE PROPHESIED HE WOULD.
BUT I'VE ALSO HEARD THAT A LOT OF PEOPLE SAW JESUS--ALIVE. I HOPE I CAN FIND SOMEONE IN JERUSALEM WHO DID.

I'M SEEKING THE TRUTH--BUT IT WILL TAKE A SIGN FROM GOD TO MAKE ME BELIEVE THAT JESUS' DISCIPLES SPEAK IT.

Like Tongues of Fire! From Acts 2:1-38

IN THAT SACRED MOMENT JESUS' FOLLOWERS ARE FILLED WITH STRENGTH AND COURAGE THEY HAVE NEVER KNOWN. RUSHING OUT OF THE UPPER ROOM AND INTO THE STREET BELOW, THEY BEGIN TO PREACH -- EACH IN A DIFFERENT LANGUAGE AS THE SPIRIT OF GOD DIRECTS.

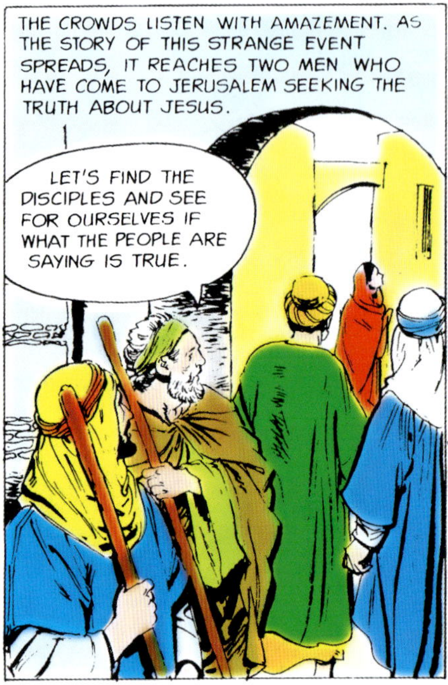

THE CROWDS LISTEN WITH AMAZEMENT. AS THE STORY OF THIS STRANGE EVENT SPREADS, IT REACHES TWO MEN WHO HAVE COME TO JERUSALEM SEEKING THE TRUTH ABOUT JESUS.

LET'S FIND THE DISCIPLES AND SEE FOR OURSELVES IF WHAT THE PEOPLE ARE SAYING IS TRUE.

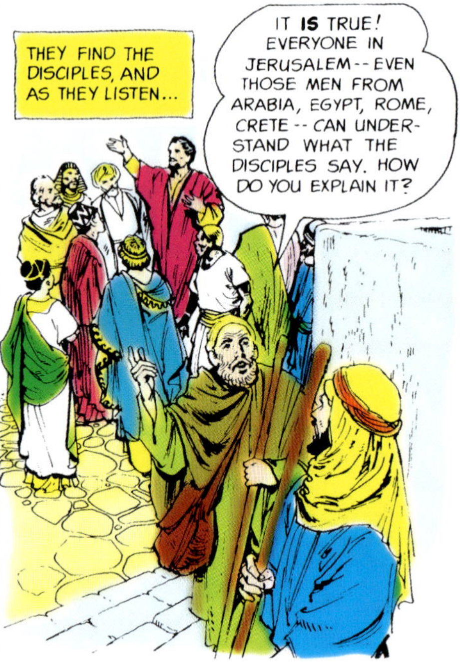

THEY FIND THE DISCIPLES, AND AS THEY LISTEN...

IT **IS** TRUE! EVERYONE IN JERUSALEM -- EVEN THOSE MEN FROM ARABIA, EGYPT, ROME, CRETE -- CAN UNDERSTAND WHAT THE DISCIPLES SAY. HOW DO YOU EXPLAIN IT?

IN ANSWER TO THIS INSULT, PETER SPEAKS OUT FOR ALL THE DISCIPLES.

WE ARE NOT DRUNK! WE ARE FILLED WITH THE HOLY SPIRIT AS THE PROPHET JOEL PROPHESIED. YOU MEN OF JERUSALEM, YOU CRUCIFIED JESUS, THE CHOSEN ONE OF GOD. BUT GOD RAISED HIM FROM THE DEAD, AND WE ARE WITNESSES TO THAT RESURRECTION!

THIS BOLD CHARGE CUTS DEEP INTO THE HEARTS OF THE PEOPLE, FOR THEY REMEMBER HOW THEY CALLED FOR JESUS' CRUCIFIXION.

REPENT OF YOUR SINS, AND BE BAPTIZED IN THE NAME OF JESUS CHRIST. THEN YOU SHALL RECEIVE THE GIFT OF THE HOLY SPIRIT AS WE HAVE!

YOU SAID IT WOULD TAKE A SIGN FROM GOD TO CONVINCE YOU THAT JESUS' DISCIPLES SPEAK THE TRUTH. WHAT DO YOU SAY NOW?

Three Thousand in a Day

From Acts 2:38—3:7

BEFORE THE DAY OF PENTECOST IS OVER, THREE THOUSAND PEOPLE ARE BAPTIZED. AND AS THE DAYS PASS MORE AND MORE JOIN THE GROUP OF JESUS' FOLLOWERS. THE UPPER ROOM IS NOT LARGE ENOUGH TO HOLD THE CROWDS, SO PEOPLE MEET IN HOMES.
I'VE BROUGHT SOME FRIENDS WHO WANT TO LEARN ABOUT JESUS.
COME IN-- YOU ARE WELCOME.
HAVE YOU HEARD-- THE POOR WIDOW WE TALKED WITH NEEDS FOOD FOR HER CHILDREN.
I'LL GIVE THE APOSTLES SOME MONEY TO HELP HER.
THE FOLLOWERS OF JESUS ARE SO HAPPY WORSHIPING TOGETHER AND TAKING CARE OF ONE ANOTHER'S NEEDS THAT SOON ALL JERUSALEM IS TALKING ABOUT THEM.
WHAT DO YOU MAKE OF THESE FRIENDS OF JESUS?
I DON'T UNDERSTAND THEM--BUT I WISH I COULD BE AS HAPPY AS THEY ARE.

ONE AFTERNOON WHEN PETER AND JOHN GO TO THE TEMPLE FOR PRAYER THEY FIND A LAME MAN BEGGING AT THE BEAUTIFUL GATE.
HAVE MERCY-- A COIN FOR THE POOR.

LOOK AT US!
MAYBE **BOTH** OF THEM WILL GIVE ME SOMETHING...

I HAVE NO MONEY, BUT I'LL GIVE YOU WHAT I HAVE. IN THE NAME OF JESUS CHRIST, RISE UP AND WALK!

WALK? THE MAN WHO HAS NEVER TAKEN A STEP IN HIS LIFE CANNOT BELIEVE WHAT HE HAS HEARD. BUT AS PETER REACHES OUT HIS HAND TO HIM, THE MAN STRETCHES FORTH HIS OWN...

Miracle at the Gate From Acts 3:7–4:17

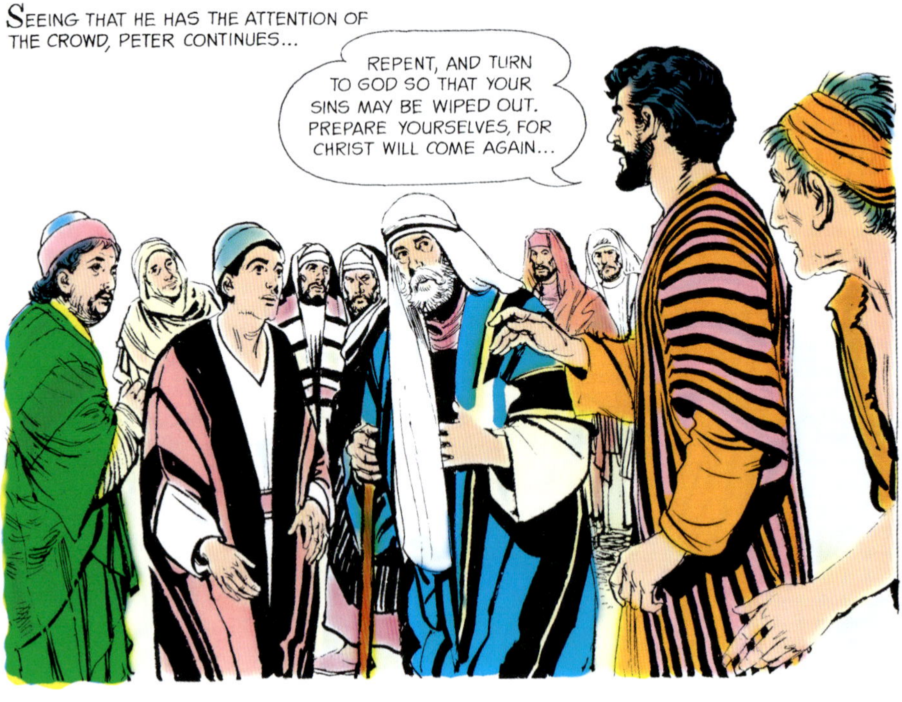

SEEING THAT HE HAS THE ATTENTION OF THE CROWD, PETER CONTINUES...

REPENT, AND TURN TO GOD SO THAT YOUR SINS MAY BE WIPED OUT. PREPARE YOURSELVES, FOR CHRIST WILL COME AGAIN...

AT THE BACK OF THE CROWD THE PRIESTS LISTEN. THEY ARE ANGRY—AND THEIR ANGER INCREASES AS THEY WATCH THE GROWING INTEREST OF THE PEOPLE.
HE MUST BE STOPPED AT ONCE--OR HE'LL HAVE ALL OF JERUSALEM BELIEVING THAT JESUS ROSE FROM THE DEAD.
WITH THE HELP OF THE CAPTAIN OF THE TEMPLE GUARDS, THE PRIESTS PUSH THEIR WAY THROUGH THE CROWDS.
YOU ARE UNDER ARREST!
WITHOUT ANOTHER WORD, PETER AND JOHN ARE MARCHED AWAY TO PRISON--BUT ALREADY FIVE THOUSAND MEN HAVE DECLARED THEIR BELIEF IN JESUS.
THE NEXT MORNING THEY ARE BROUGHT BEFORE THE SANHEDRIN, THE SAME JEWISH COURT THAT CONDEMNED JESUS TO DEATH. BESIDE THEM--PERFECTLY WELL--STANDS THE MAN WHO HAD BEEN LAME FROM BIRTH.
BY WHAT POWER AND IN WHOSE NAME HAVE YOU HEALED THIS MAN?

FILLED WITH THE HOLY SPIRIT, PETER SPEAKS OUT COURAGEOUSLY.
LET IT BE KNOWN TO YOU, AND ALL THE PEOPLE OF ISRAEL -- THIS MAN WAS HEALED BY THE NAME OF JESUS CHRIST OF NAZARETH, WHOM **YOU** CRUCIFIED!
THE COURT IS STUNNED. PETER AND JOHN ARE UNEDUCATED FISHERMEN, YET THEY SPEAK AND ACT WITH AUTHORITY AND POWER.
TAKE THEM AWAY --UNTIL WE CALL FOR THEM AGAIN.
THE MINUTE THE PRISONERS ARE OUT OF SIGHT, THE COURT HOLDS A MEETING.
EVERYONE KNOWS A MIRACLE HAS TAKEN PLACE. WE CANNOT DENY IT, BUT WE MUST KEEP THE NEWS FROM SPREADING. WHAT CAN WE DO?
TELL THESE "PREACHERS" THAT IF THEY SPEAK AGAIN IN THE NAME OF JESUS THEY WILL BE PUT TO DEATH AS HE WAS!

The Pretenders

From Acts 4:18—5:18

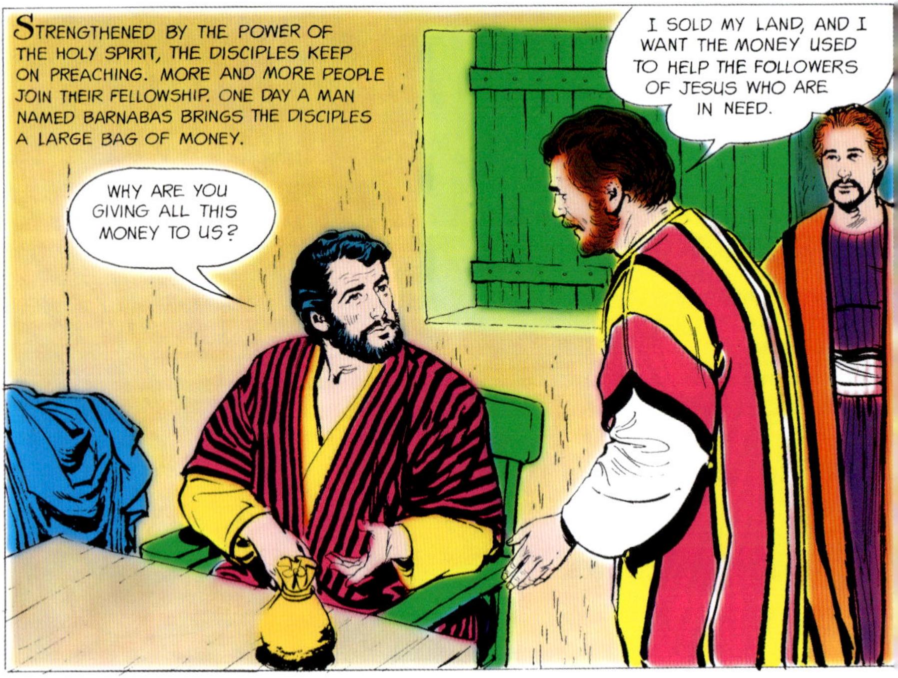

STRENGTHENED BY THE POWER OF THE HOLY SPIRIT, THE DISCIPLES KEEP ON PREACHING. MORE AND MORE PEOPLE JOIN THEIR FELLOWSHIP. ONE DAY A MAN NAMED BARNABAS BRINGS THE DISCIPLES A LARGE BAG OF MONEY.

I SOLD MY LAND, AND I WANT THE MONEY USED TO HELP THE FOLLOWERS OF JESUS WHO ARE IN NEED.

WHY ARE YOU GIVING ALL THIS MONEY TO US?

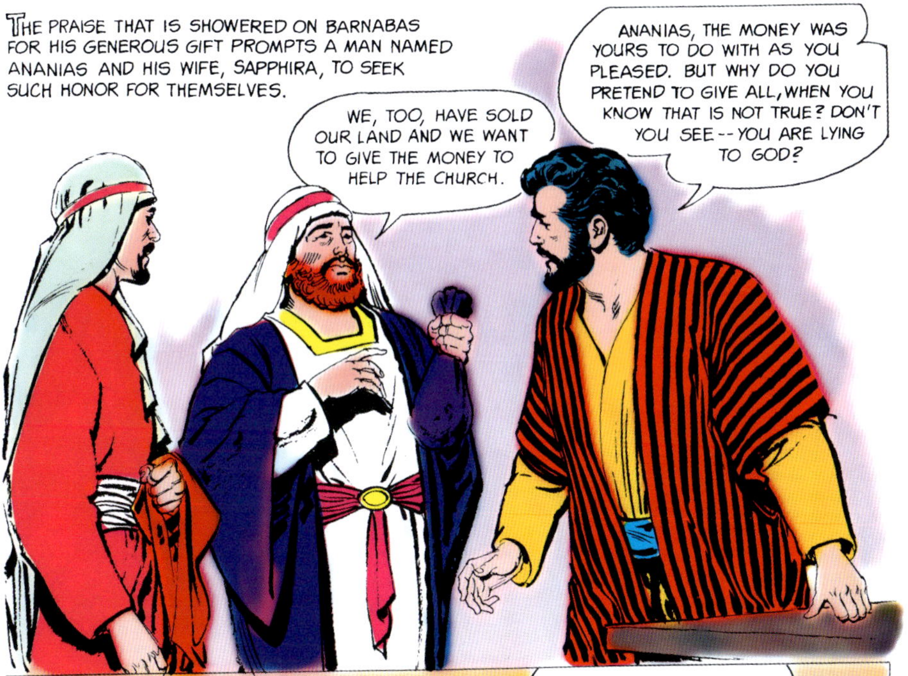

THE PRAISE THAT IS SHOWERED ON BARNABAS FOR HIS GENEROUS GIFT PROMPTS A MAN NAMED ANANIAS AND HIS WIFE, SAPPHIRA, TO SEEK SUCH HONOR FOR THEMSELVES.

WE, TOO, HAVE SOLD OUR LAND AND WE WANT TO GIVE THE MONEY TO HELP THE CHURCH.

ANANIAS, THE MONEY WAS YOURS TO DO WITH AS YOU PLEASED. BUT WHY DO YOU PRETEND TO GIVE ALL, WHEN YOU KNOW THAT IS NOT TRUE? DON'T YOU SEE--YOU ARE LYING TO GOD?

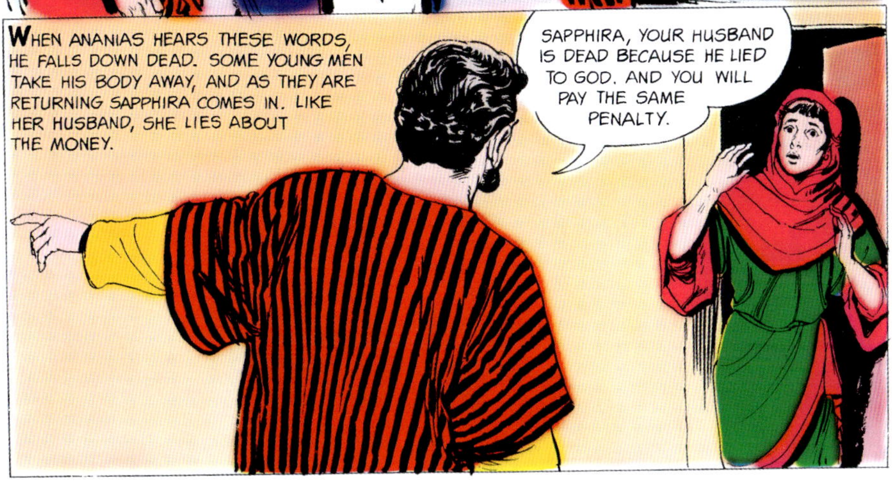

WHEN ANANIAS HEARS THESE WORDS, HE FALLS DOWN DEAD. SOME YOUNG MEN TAKE HIS BODY AWAY, AND AS THEY ARE RETURNING SAPPHIRA COMES IN. LIKE HER HUSBAND, SHE LIES ABOUT THE MONEY.

SAPPHIRA, YOUR HUSBAND IS DEAD BECAUSE HE LIED TO GOD. AND YOU WILL PAY THE SAME PENALTY.

IN SPITE OF THREATS, THE DISCIPLES KEEP ON HEALING IN THE NAME OF JESUS. THE PRIESTS WATCH--ANGRY BUT HELPLESS--AS FAMILIES BRING THEIR SICK ONES OUT INTO THE STREETS, WAITING FOR THE DISCIPLES TO PASS BY AND HEAL THEM.

THE FAME OF THE DISCIPLES SPREADS--AND SOON PEOPLE FROM THE TOWNS ROUND ABOUT CROWD INTO JERUSALEM, BEGGING TO BE HEALED. AT LAST THE PRIESTS CAN STAND IT NO LONGER. IN A FIT OF RAGE THEY HAVE THE DISCIPLES ARRESTED AND THROWN INTO JAIL.

Missing Prisoners

From Acts 5:19–6:10

THE NEXT MORNING THE HIGH PRIEST CALLS THE JEWISH COURT INTO SESSION AND ORDERS THE DISCIPLES BROUGHT BEFORE IT. WHEN THE OFFICERS RETURN...
THE PRISON IS LOCKED AND THE GUARDS ARE ON DUTY! BUT WHEN WE OPENED THE DOORS THERE WAS NO ONE THERE!

NOT THERE? WHERE ARE THEY?

AT THAT MOMENT A PRIEST ENTERS THE ROOM.
THE MEN YOU PUT IN JAIL LAST NIGHT ARE IN THE TEMPLE TEACHING ABOUT JESUS!

THE HIGH PRIEST ORDERS THE DISCIPLES BROUGHT TO THE COURT AT ONCE.
DIDN'T WE WARN YOU NOT TO PREACH ABOUT JESUS?

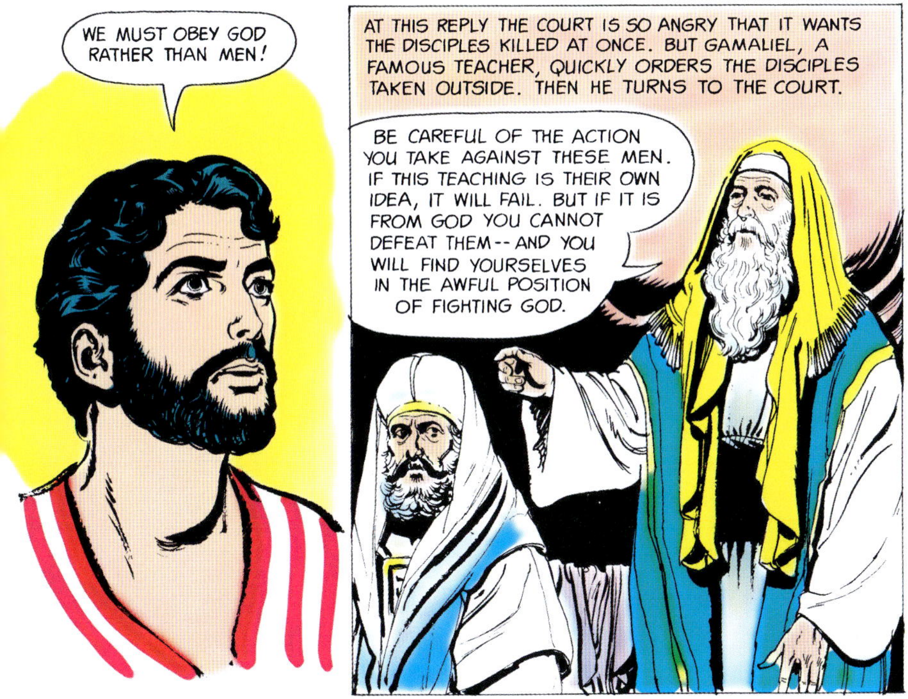

WE MUST OBEY GOD RATHER THAN MEN!

AT THIS REPLY THE COURT IS SO ANGRY THAT IT WANTS THE DISCIPLES KILLED AT ONCE. BUT GAMALIEL, A FAMOUS TEACHER, QUICKLY ORDERS THE DISCIPLES TAKEN OUTSIDE. THEN HE TURNS TO THE COURT.

BE CAREFUL OF THE ACTION YOU TAKE AGAINST THESE MEN. IF THIS TEACHING IS THEIR OWN IDEA, IT WILL FAIL. BUT IF IT IS FROM GOD YOU CANNOT DEFEAT THEM -- AND YOU WILL FIND YOURSELVES IN THE AWFUL POSITION OF FIGHTING GOD.

THE COURT IS FORCED TO ADMIT THE WISDOM OF THIS ADVICE. ANGRILY IT ORDERS THE DISCIPLES BEATEN, THEN RELEASES THEM WITH A THREAT OF MORE PUNISHMENT IF THEY CONTINUE PREACHING ABOUT JESUS.

IN SPITE OF THREATS THE DISCIPLES GO ON PREACHING AND HEALING. THE NUMBER OF FOLLOWERS INCREASES SO MUCH THAT THE TWELVE DISCIPLES DECIDE OTHERS MUST BE CHOSEN TO HELP WITH THE WORK. SEVEN DEACONS ARE SELECTED.

ONE OF THEM -- STEPHEN -- IS SOON RECOGNIZED AS A FINE PREACHER.

HIS FORMER FRIENDS IN THE SYNAGOGUE CHALLENGE HIM TO A DEBATE ABOUT JESUS. TO THEIR EMBARRASSMENT THEY FIND THEY ARE NO MATCH FOR STEPHEN'S WISDOM AND ABILITY TO DEFEND HIS FAITH. SECRETLY THEY PLOT THEIR REVENGE.

WE MUST BE CAREFUL NOT TO TURN THE PEOPLE AGAINST US.

RIGHT -- BUT IF WE HANDLE IT PROPERLY WE CAN USE THE PEOPLE THEMSELVES TO HELP US DESTROY STEPHEN.

Martyr for Christ

From Acts 6:11–8:4

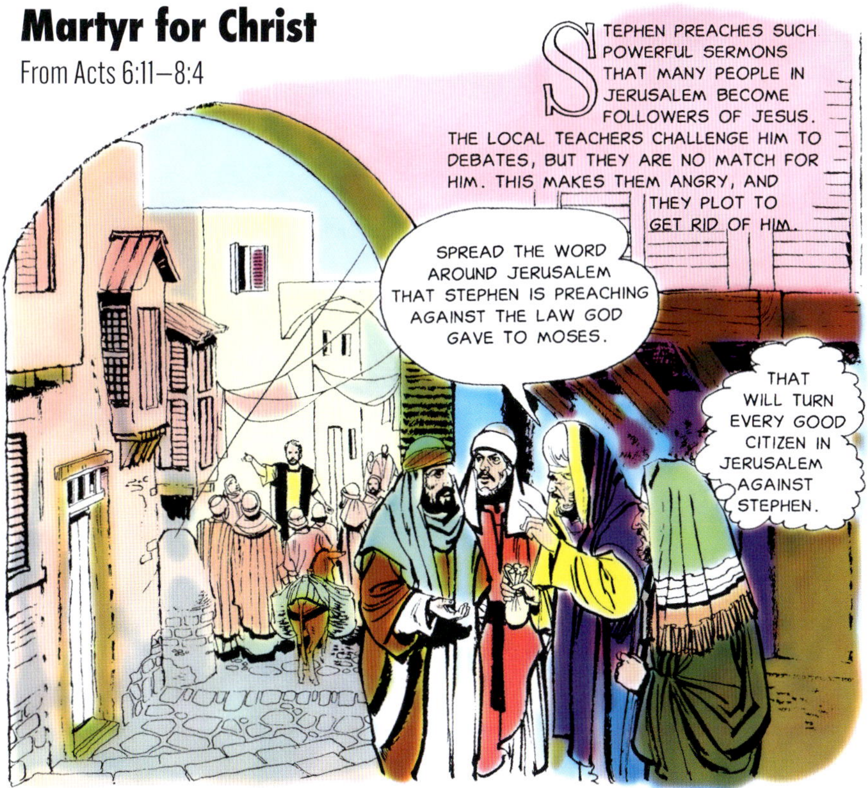

STEPHEN PREACHES SUCH POWERFUL SERMONS THAT MANY PEOPLE IN JERUSALEM BECOME FOLLOWERS OF JESUS. THE LOCAL TEACHERS CHALLENGE HIM TO DEBATES, BUT THEY ARE NO MATCH FOR HIM. THIS MAKES THEM ANGRY, AND THEY PLOT TO GET RID OF HIM.

SPREAD THE WORD AROUND JERUSALEM THAT STEPHEN IS PREACHING AGAINST THE LAW GOD GAVE TO MOSES.

THAT WILL TURN EVERY GOOD CITIZEN IN JERUSALEM AGAINST STEPHEN.

THE PLOT WORKS -- STEPHEN IS ARRESTED AND BROUGHT BEFORE THE SANHEDRIN, THE SAME COURT THAT CONDEMNED JESUS TO DEATH.

THE COURT RISES UP IN RAGE, BUT STEPHEN CONTINUES.
I SEE THE HEAVENS OPEN AND JESUS STANDING AT THE RIGHT HAND OF GOD!
AT THIS THE MEMBERS OF THE COURT, LIKE A PACK OF SAVAGE BEASTS, SEIZE STEPHEN AND RUSH HIM OUTSIDE THE CITY. THERE THE PAID WITNESSES THROW THEIR OUTER GARMENTS ON THE GROUND AND ASK A YOUNG MAN NAMED PAUL TO GUARD THEM. AS STEPHEN IS STONED HE PRAYS, "LORD JESUS, RECEIVE MY SPIRIT." THEN WITH HIS LAST BREATH...
LORD, FORGIVE THEM FOR THIS SIN.
THE STONING OF STEPHEN SERVES AS A SIGNAL FOR THE ENEMIES OF JESUS TO ATTACK ALL OF HIS FOLLOWERS. BEFORE THE DAY IS OVER PAUL BEGINS RAIDING HOMES AND DRAGGING MEN AND WOMEN OFF TO PRISON.
NO! MY CHILDREN!
SOON THERE WON'T BE MANY FRIENDS OF JESUS LEFT IN JERUSALEM—THEN THE WHOLE MOVEMENT WILL DIE OUT.

REMEMBERING THE APOSTLES' STRANGE ESCAPE FROM PRISON, THE PERSECUTORS SEEM AFRAID TO ARREST THEM. BUT RAIDS AGAINST THE OTHER DISCIPLES CONTINUE, AND THEY ARE FORCED TO FLEE FOR THEIR LIVES.
WE MUST ESCAPE AT ONCE. I'M NOT A COWARD, BUT MY FAMILY--
JESUS SAID THAT IF WE WERE PERSECUTED IN ONE CITY WE SHOULD FLEE TO ANOTHER.
TWO BIG CARAVANS ARE LEAVING BY THE NORTH GATE TOMORROW MORNING. IF WE'RE CAREFUL WE CAN JOIN THEM AND NOT BE SEEN.
EARLY THE NEXT MORNING TRADERS LEAD THEIR CAMEL TRAINS OUT OF THE CITY, AND IN THEIR MIDST...
WHEREVER WE GO WE'LL TAKE OUR FAITH IN JESUS WITH US.
AND AS WE TEACH OTHERS WE'LL BE HELPING TO SPREAD THE GOSPEL AS JESUS ASKED US TO DO.
AND SO, BY DRIVING JESUS' FRIENDS OUT OF JERUSALEM, LOCAL LEADERS, UNKNOWINGLY, CAUSE HIS TEACHINGS TO BE SPREAD THROUGHOUT ALL PALESTINE--EVEN AMONG THEIR ENEMIES, THE SAMARITANS!

Simon, the Magician

From Acts 8:5-26

TO ESCAPE PERSECUTION AT THE HANDS OF THE RELIGIOUS LEADERS, THOUSANDS OF JESUS' FOLLOWERS FLEE FROM JERUSALEM. PHILIP, ONE OF THE DEACONS OF THE JERUSALEM CHURCH, GOES NORTH TO SAMARIA.

SIMON, THE MOST FAMOUS MAGICIAN IN SAMARIA, HURRIES OFF TO FIND PHILIP.

I THOUGHT I KNEW ALL THE TRICKS OF MAGIC.

WHEN HE FINDS PHILIP HE WATCHES WITH AMAZEMENT THE MIRACLES OF HEALING. BUT HE ALSO LISTENS TO WHAT PHILIP SAYS, AND AFTER A WHILE...

I BELIEVE IN JESUS, TOO. BAPTIZE ME, AND LET ME GO WITH YOU TO LEARN MORE.

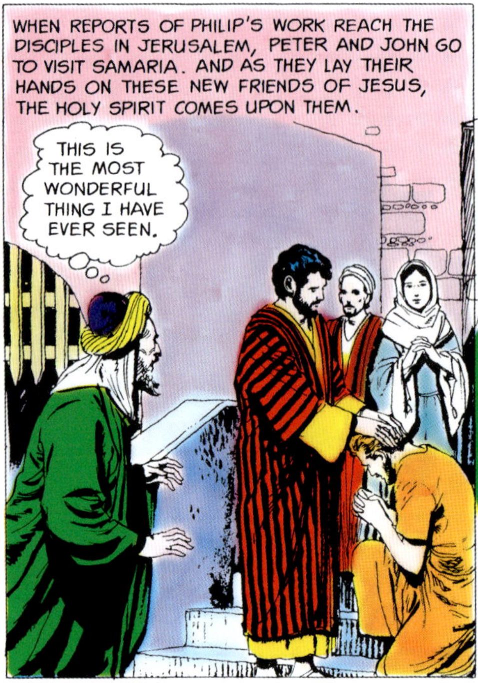

WHEN REPORTS OF PHILIP'S WORK REACH THE DISCIPLES IN JERUSALEM, PETER AND JOHN GO TO VISIT SAMARIA. AND AS THEY LAY THEIR HANDS ON THESE NEW FRIENDS OF JESUS, THE HOLY SPIRIT COMES UPON THEM.

THIS IS THE MOST WONDERFUL THING I HAVE EVER SEEN.

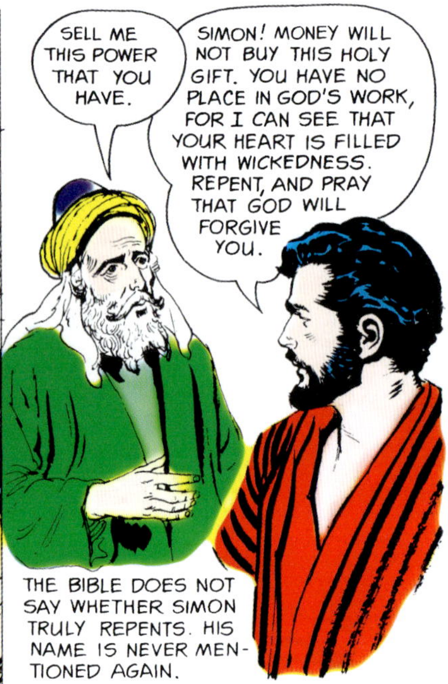

SELL ME THIS POWER THAT YOU HAVE.

SIMON! MONEY WILL NOT BUY THIS HOLY GIFT. YOU HAVE NO PLACE IN GOD'S WORK, FOR I CAN SEE THAT YOUR HEART IS FILLED WITH WICKEDNESS. REPENT, AND PRAY THAT GOD WILL FORGIVE YOU.

THE BIBLE DOES NOT SAY WHETHER SIMON TRULY REPENTS. HIS NAME IS NEVER MENTIONED AGAIN.

On the Gaza Road

From Acts 8:26-40; 9:32-35

AGAIN PHILIP OBEYS. NEARING THE CHARIOT, HE HEARS A MAN READING FROM THE SCRIPTURES.
"HE WAS LED AS A SHEEP TO THE SLAUGHTER."
DO YOU UNDERSTAND WHAT THE PROPHET ISAIAH IS SAYING?
HOW CAN I UNLESS SOMEONE HELPS ME? WILL YOU?
EAGERLY PHILIP GETS INTO THE CHARIOT. THE MAN INTRODUCES HIMSELF AS TREASURER FOR CANDACE, QUEEN OF ETHIOPIA. THEN HE TURNS BACK TO THE SCROLL.
IS THE PROPHET TALKING ABOUT HIMSELF--OR SOMEONE ELSE?
ABOUT JESUS CHRIST, THE SON OF GOD. HIS ENEMIES CRUCIFIED HIM, BUT GOD RAISED HIM FROM THE DEAD.

AS THEY RIDE ALONG PHILIP EXPLAINS THAT GOD LOVED THE WORLD SO MUCH THAT HE SENT HIS SON JESUS TO DIE FOR OUR SINS, AND WHOEVER TRUSTS IN HIM WILL LIVE FOREVER WITH GOD.
I BELIEVE IN JESUS, AND I'M SORRY FOR EVERYTHING WRONG I HAVE DONE. IS THERE ANY REASON WHY I CANNOT BE BAPTIZED AND BECOME ONE OF HIS FOLLOWERS?
I'M SURE THAT'S WHAT GOD SENT ME HERE TO DO.
SO THE MAN FROM ETHIOPIA IS BAPTIZED... AND THEN HE CONTINUES HIS JOURNEY, EAGER TO TELL THE GOOD NEWS ABOUT JESUS TO HIS OWN PEOPLE.
PHILIP GOES NORTH, PREACHING IN THE TOWNS ALONG THE RIM OF THE MEDITERRANEAN SEA. IN CAESAREA, THE ROMAN CAPITAL IN PALESTINE, HE MAKES HIS HOME.
ABOUT THIS TIME A MIRACULOUS THING HAPPENS--PAUL, WHO HAS BEEN PERSECUTING JESUS' FRIENDS, HAS A WONDERFUL EXPERIENCE. ON THE WAY TO DAMASCUS, JESUS APPEARS TO HIM. PAUL KNOWS THAT JESUS IS THE SAVIOR WHOM GOD RAISED FROM THE DEAD. SO, INSTEAD OF PERSECUTING JESUS' FOLLOWERS, PAUL BECOMES A FOLLOWER, TOO.
WHEN THE DISCIPLES HEAR THIS THEY REJOICE, FOR NOW THEY CAN TRAVEL ALL OVER PALESTINE TEACHING AND HEALING IN THE NAME OF JESUS WITHOUT FEAR OF PAUL ARRESTING THEM.
Sea of Galilee
CAESAREA
JOPPA
LYDDA
JERUSALEM
GAZA
Dead Sea
MEDITERRANEAN SEA

AENEAS STANDS UP. HE LOOKS IN AWE AT HIS STRONG ARMS AND LEGS.

WHEN THE PEOPLE SEE AENEAS -- WELL AND STRONG -- THEY BELIEVE IN JESUS, TOO. PETER STAYS IN LYDDA, PREACHING, UNTIL ONE DAY TWO MEN FROM THE SEAPORT OF JOPPA ARRIVE IN THE CITY.

WHERE'S PETER? WE MUST FIND HIM AT ONCE!

Mission to Joppa

From Acts 9:36–10:2

WHILE PETER IS PREACHING IN LYDDA TWO MEN FROM JOPPA COME TO HIM WITH AN URGENT REQUEST: "DORCAS, ONE OF JESUS' FOLLOWERS, JUST DIED. YOU RESTORED AENEAS' HEALTH; CAN YOU HELP DORCAS?" PETER GOES WITH THE MEN AT ONCE, AND WHEN THEY REACH JOPPA ...

HER BODY HAS BEEN PLACED IN THE ROOM UPSTAIRS.

THEY FIND DORCAS' HOUSE FILLED WITH WEEPING FRIENDS.
SHE WAS THE KINDEST PERSON I EVER KNEW. SEE THIS COAT--SHE MADE IT FOR ME.
I KNOW HOW MUCH YOU LOVED HER. NOW, IF YOU WILL PLEASE GO OUTSIDE.
ALONE, PETER KNEELS DOWN AND PRAYS. AS HE RISES HE TURNS TO THE BODY OF THE DEAD WOMAN...
DORCAS, GET UP!
INSTANTLY DORCAS OPENS HER EYES. PETER HELPS HER TO RISE, THEN HE PRESENTS HER TO THE PEOPLE WHO HAVE BEEN WAITING OUTSIDE.
GIVE THANKS TO GOD-- YOUR FRIEND IS ALIVE!

AT THE SIGHT OF DORCAS SOME OF THE WOMEN FALL ON THEIR KNEES, WEEPING FOR JOY. OTHERS RUSH OUT INTO THE STREETS TO TELL THE EXCITING NEWS.
DORCAS IS ALIVE!
SHH--PEOPLE WILL THINK YOU'RE LOSING YOUR MIND. DORCAS IS DEAD--AND EVERYONE KNOWS IT.

NO! NO! PETER, THE DISCIPLE OF JESUS, BROUGHT HER BACK TO LIFE. COME, SEE FOR YOURSELF!

NOT BELIEVING, BUT CURIOUS, THE WOMAN HURRIES TO DORCAS' HOME.
IT'S TRUE! IT'S TRUE! OH, GOD BE PRAISED!
THE NEWS SPREADS QUICKLY THROUGHOUT JOPPA, AND SOON GREAT CROWDS COME TO PETER, BEGGING TO BE TAUGHT ABOUT JESUS. PETER CONTINUES TO PREACH IN JOPPA UNTIL...

ONE DAY A STRANGE THING HAPPENS IN THE HOME OF CORNELIUS, A ROMAN CENTURION LIVING IN THE SEACOAST CITY OF CAESAREA, SOME THIRTY MILES NORTH. IT IS THREE O'CLOCK IN THE AFTERNOON. CORNELIUS, WHO IN HIS YEARS OF SERVICE IN PALESTINE HAS LEARNED TO WORSHIP GOD, KNEELS TO PRAY.

God, a Roman, and a Jew

From Acts 10:2—11:1

HE, TOO, HAS A VISION. AND A VOICE COMMANDS HIM: "GET UP, PETER; KILL AND EAT."

NEVER, LORD. IN ALL MY LIFE I HAVE NEVER EATEN ANYTHING THAT THE JEWISH LAW CALLS UNCLEAN.

THE VOICE REPLIES: "YOU MUST NOT CALL WHAT GOD HAS CLEANSED UNCLEAN." ALL THIS IS REPEATED THREE TIMES; THEN THE VISION DISAPPEARS. WHILE PETER IS WONDERING WHAT IT MEANS THE HOLY SPIRIT SPEAKS TO HIM: "THREE MEN ARE HERE LOOKING FOR YOU. GO WITH THEM AND HAVE NO DOUBTS, FOR I HAVE SENT THEM TO YOU."

PETER HURRIES DOWNSTAIRS -- AND FINDS THREE MEN AT THE GATE INQUIRING FOR HIM.

I AM THE MAN YOU ARE LOOKING FOR. WHAT DO YOU WANT?

CORNELIUS, A ROMAN CENTURION WHO WORSHIPS GOD, WAS COMMANDED BY AN ANGEL TO SEND FOR YOU.

THE NEXT DAY PETER AND SIX OF HIS FRIENDS SET OUT WITH THE THREE MEN FOR CAESAREA. AS THEY ENTER THE HOME OF CORNELIUS, THE ROMAN CENTURION FALLS ON HIS KNEES TO WORSHIP PETER.

NO -- NO -- I AM A MAN LIKE YOURSELF.

THEN PETER TELLS THEM THAT JESUS WAS THE SAVIOR SENT FROM GOD TO GIVE ETERNAL LIFE TO ALL WHO BELIEVE IN HIM. WHEN PETER SEES THAT THE HOLY SPIRIT HAS COME TO THE GENTILES, HE HAS HIS CHRISTIAN FRIENDS BAPTIZE THEM.

Angel—Open Gate

From Acts 11:1–12:14

AND AS IT DOES, THE ANGER OF THE LOCAL LEADERS GROWS. TO WIN THEIR FAVOR, KING HEROD AGRIPPA BEGINS TO PERSECUTE JESUS' FOLLOWERS.

ARREST THE DISCIPLE CALLED JAMES. CHARGE HIM WITH STIRRING UP TROUBLE AND PUT HIM TO DEATH-- AT ONCE!

SO JAMES, ONE OF THE FOUR FISHERMEN WHO LEFT THEIR NETS TO FOLLOW JESUS, IS SLAIN TO SATISFY A WICKED KING'S STRUGGLE FOR POWER.

THIS PLEASES THE RELIGIOUS LEADERS WHO CONDEMNED JESUS TO DEATH. EAGER TO GAIN MORE OF THEIR FAVOR, HEROD ORDERS PETER ARRESTED AND PUT IN PRISON--TO BE EXECUTED AFTER THE FEAST OF THE PASSOVER.

CHAIN EACH HAND TO A GUARD. KEEP FOUR SOLDIERS ON WATCH AT ALL TIMES. THIS PRISONER **MUST NOT** ESCAPE!

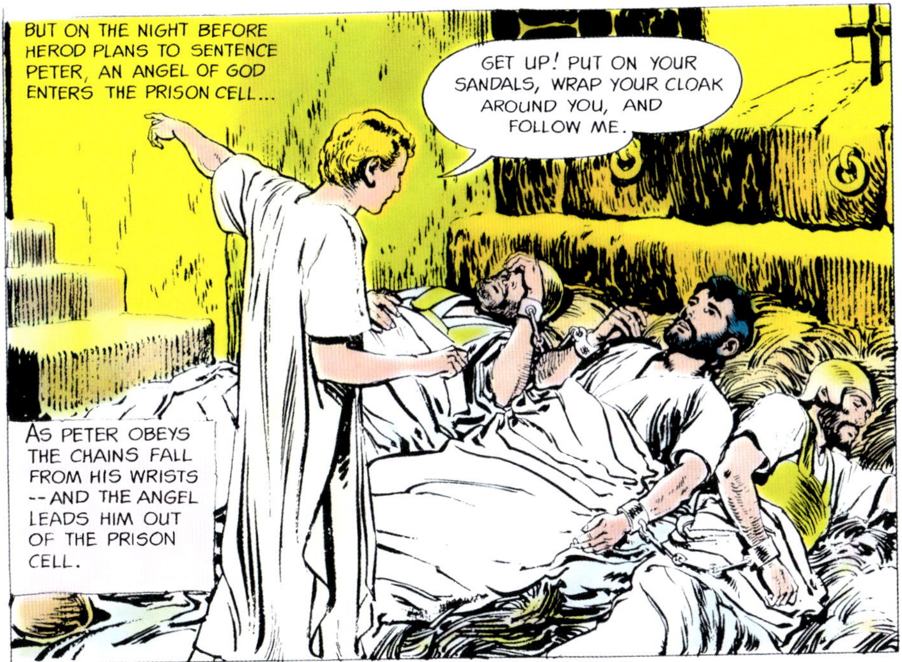

BUT ON THE NIGHT BEFORE HEROD PLANS TO SENTENCE PETER, AN ANGEL OF GOD ENTERS THE PRISON CELL...

GET UP! PUT ON YOUR SANDALS, WRAP YOUR CLOAK AROUND YOU, AND FOLLOW ME.

AS PETER OBEYS THE CHAINS FALL FROM HIS WRISTS -- AND THE ANGEL LEADS HIM OUT OF THE PRISON CELL.

WHEN THEY APPROACH THE GREAT IRON GATE IN THE PRISON WALL, IT OPENS! THEY GO OUT INTO THE CITY STREETS, AND -- SUDDENLY -- THE ANGEL VANISHES!

Fall of a Tyrant

From Acts 12:14-24

THE FRIENDS OF PETER REJOICE AND THANK GOD FOR HIS ESCAPE, BUT THE NEXT MORNING WHEN HEROD DISCOVERS THAT HIS PRISONER IS GONE--

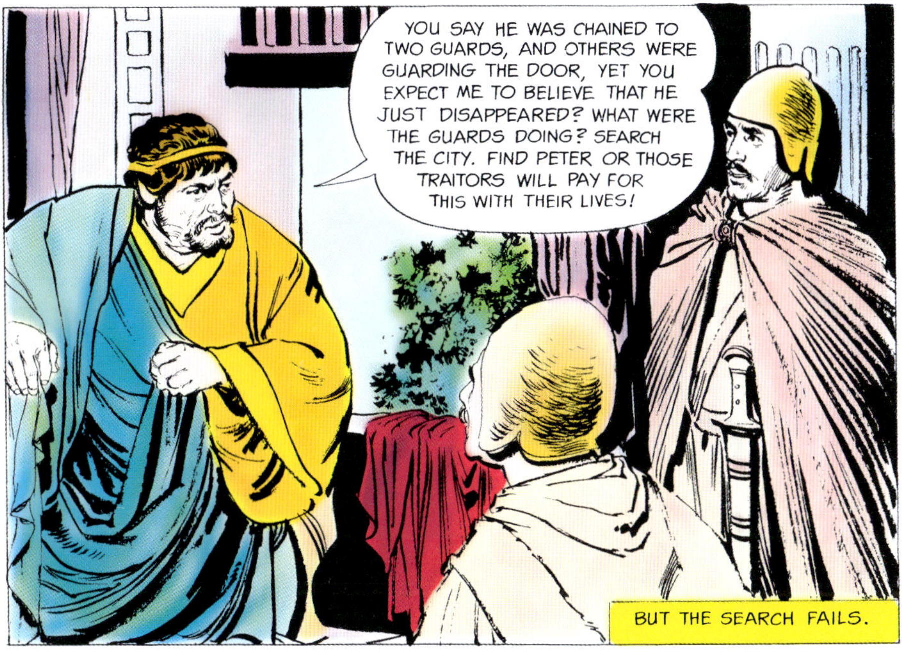

YOU SAY HE WAS CHAINED TO TWO GUARDS, AND OTHERS WERE GUARDING THE DOOR, YET YOU EXPECT ME TO BELIEVE THAT HE JUST DISAPPEARED? WHAT WERE THE GUARDS DOING? SEARCH THE CITY. FIND PETER OR THOSE TRAITORS WILL PAY FOR THIS WITH THEIR LIVES!

BUT THE SEARCH FAILS.

A FEW DAYS LATER HEROD APPEARS AT A PUBLIC CELEBRATION IN CAESAREA. THERE, DRESSED IN A DAZZLING ROBE OF SILVER, HE GOES OUT AND SPEAKS TO THE PEOPLE. TO FLATTER HIM, THEY SHOUT:

IT IS THE VOICE OF A GOD--NOT A MAN!

HEROD ACCEPTS THE PRAISE WHICH SHOULD HAVE BEEN GIVEN ONLY TO GOD. SUDDENLY GOD STRIKES HIM DOWN, AND A FEW DAYS LATER HE DIES.

WITH THE DEATH OF HEROD, THE PERSECUTION OF THE CHURCH STOPS FOR A TIME. THE GOOD NEWS OF JESUS CHRIST CONTINUES TO SPREAD THROUGHOUT THE LAND OF THE JEWS...

The Story of Paul

From Acts 7:58–8:4; 9:1-3A; 22:3

Adventurer for Christ

BOLDLY HE FACES ANGRY MOBS... CROSSES MOUNTAINS... AND SAILS THE STORMY SEAS TO PREACH THE GOOD NEWS THAT JESUS IS THE SON OF GOD AND SAVIOR OF THE WORLD.

THE EXCITING STORY OF THIS GREAT MISSIONARY BEGINS LONG AGO...

A FEW YEARS AFTER THE BIRTH OF JESUS PAUL* IS BORN IN TARSUS. THE SON OF GOOD JEWISH PARENTS, HE IS BROUGHT UP TO WORSHIP AND OBEY GOD.

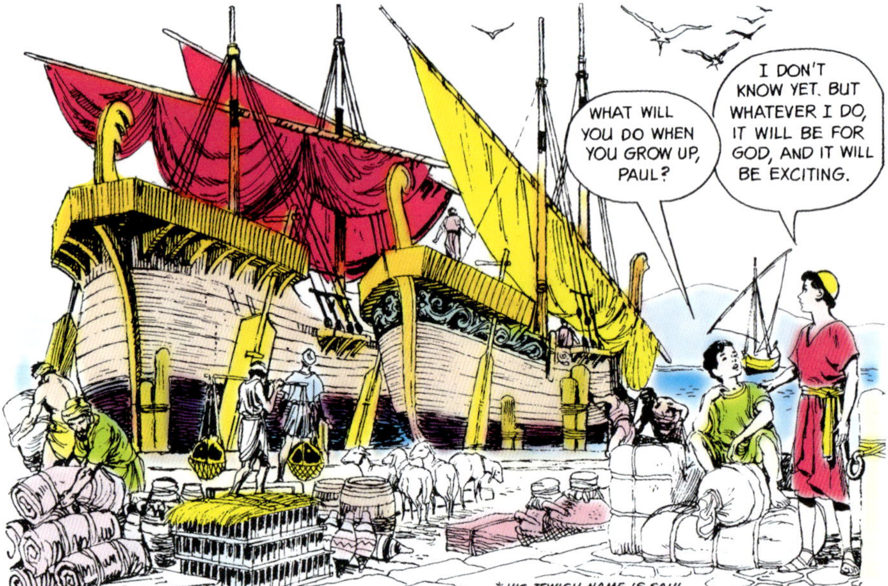

WHAT WILL YOU DO WHEN YOU GROW UP, PAUL?

I DON'T KNOW YET. BUT WHATEVER I DO, IT WILL BE FOR GOD, AND IT WILL BE EXCITING.

*HIS JEWISH NAME IS SAUL.

HE TAKES THE FIRST STEP TOWARD MAKING HIS DREAM COME TRUE WHEN HE GOES TO JERUSALEM TO STUDY. THERE HE MEETS SOME OF THE SAME TEACHERS THAT JESUS TALKED WITH ONLY A FEW YEARS BEFORE.

IN TIME PAUL BECOMES THE MOST BRILLIANT PUPIL OF THE FAMOUS TEACHER, GAMALIEL. TOGETHER THEY DISCUSS THE SCRIPTURES -- ESPECIALLY THE PARTS THAT TELL ABOUT THE COMING OF THE SAVIOR.

BUT LIKE MOST JEWISH LEADERS, PAUL REFUSES TO ACCEPT JESUS AS THE SAVIOR FOR WHOM THE JEWS ARE WAITING. WHEN THEY STONE STEPHEN, ONE OF JESUS' FOLLOWERS, PAUL STANDS BY-- WATCHING.
ANY MAN WHO FOLLOWS JESUS DESERVES TO DIE!
PAUL SOON BEGINS HIS OWN ATTACK ON JESUS' FOLLOWERS. HE RAIDS THEIR HOMES AND DRAGS THEM OFF TO BE QUESTIONED, PUNISHED, EVEN PUT TO DEATH.
NO! NO! MY CHILDREN!
THE FOLLOWERS OF JESUS FLEE FOR THEIR LIVES. WHEN PAUL LEARNS THAT THEY ARE SPREADING THEIR TEACHING WHEREVER THEY GO, HE IS EVEN MORE FURIOUS.
THEY MUST BE STOPPED BEFORE THEY STIR UP PEOPLE EVERYWHERE. ALREADY THEY ARE AS FAR NORTH AS DAMASCUS.
WHAT CAN WE DO?

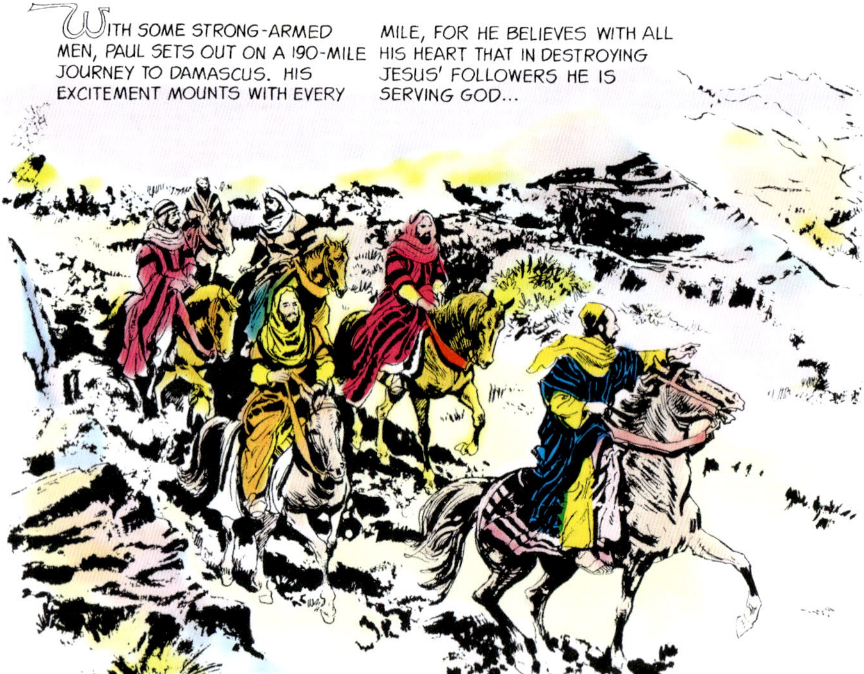

WITH SOME STRONG-ARMED MEN, PAUL SETS OUT ON A 190-MILE JOURNEY TO DAMASCUS. HIS EXCITEMENT MOUNTS WITH EVERY MILE, FOR HE BELIEVES WITH ALL HIS HEART THAT IN DESTROYING JESUS' FOLLOWERS HE IS SERVING GOD...

A Light and a Voice

From Acts 9:3-22

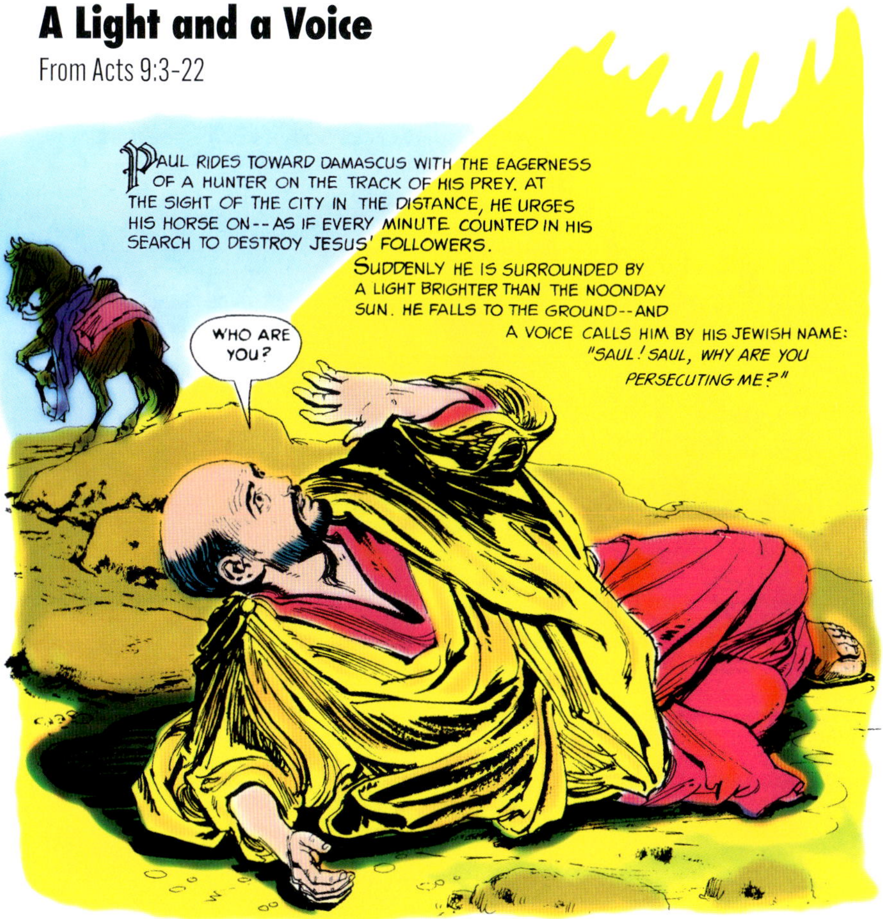

PAUL RIDES TOWARD DAMASCUS WITH THE EAGERNESS OF A HUNTER ON THE TRACK OF HIS PREY. AT THE SIGHT OF THE CITY IN THE DISTANCE, HE URGES HIS HORSE ON--AS IF EVERY MINUTE COUNTED IN HIS SEARCH TO DESTROY JESUS' FOLLOWERS.

SUDDENLY HE IS SURROUNDED BY A LIGHT BRIGHTER THAN THE NOONDAY SUN. HE FALLS TO THE GROUND--AND A VOICE CALLS HIM BY HIS JEWISH NAME: "SAUL! SAUL, WHY ARE YOU PERSECUTING ME?"

WHO ARE YOU?

THE MEN WITH PAUL ARE TERRIFIED BY WHAT HAS HAPPENED.

SO, BLIND, AND AWED BY HIS EXPERIENCE, THE ONCE-PROUD PAUL IS LED INTO DAMASCUS-- DOWN A STREET CALLED STRAIGHT.

IN DARKNESS PAUL PRAYS AND WAITS. ON THE THIRD DAY HE CALLS TO HIS HOST.

WHILE PAUL IS PRAYING, JESUS APPEARS TO ONE OF HIS FOLLOWERS IN ANOTHER PART OF THE CITY.
ANANIAS, GET UP. GO TO THE HOUSE OF JUDAS ON THE STREET CALLED STRAIGHT. ASK FOR A MAN NAMED PAUL. HE IS PRAYING, AND HE HAS SEEN YOU COMING TO RESTORE HIS SIGHT.
LORD, I HAVE HEARD OF THIS MAN AND THE EVIL HE HAS DONE TO YOUR FOLLOWERS IN JERUSALEM.
GO, FOR I HAVE CHOSEN HIM TO TAKE MY NAME BEFORE THE GENTILES, AND KINGS, AND THE CHILDREN OF ISRAEL.
ANANIAS OBEYS. AT THE HOME OF JUDAS HE IS TAKEN AT ONCE TO SEE PAUL.
ANANIAS HAS COME... JUST AS YOU SAID.
BROTHER PAUL, THE LORD JESUS HAS SENT ME TO RESTORE YOUR SIGHT.
ANANIAS LAYS HIS HANDS ON PAUL'S EYES.
PRAISE GOD! I CAN SEE AGAIN!

Man with a Mission

From Acts 9:27-30; 11:22-25

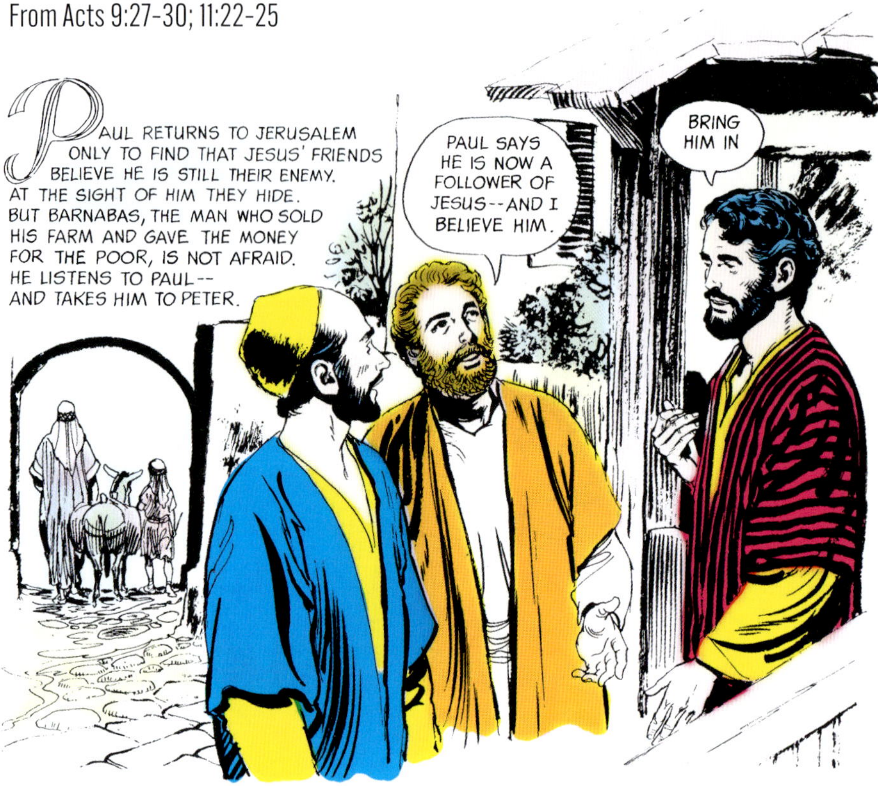

PAUL RETURNS TO JERUSALEM ONLY TO FIND THAT JESUS' FRIENDS BELIEVE HE IS STILL THEIR ENEMY. AT THE SIGHT OF HIM THEY HIDE. BUT BARNABAS, THE MAN WHO SOLD HIS FARM AND GAVE THE MONEY FOR THE POOR, IS NOT AFRAID. HE LISTENS TO PAUL--AND TAKES HIM TO PETER.

PAUL SAYS HE IS NOW A FOLLOWER OF JESUS--AND I BELIEVE HIM.

BRING HIM IN

BOLDLY PAUL TAKES HIS STAND BEFORE ALL JERUSALEM.
I BELIEVE JESUS ROSE FROM THE DEAD! I BELIEVE HE IS OUR SAVIOR!
WHAT HAS HAPPENED TO MAKE PAUL TALK LIKE THIS? MAYBE JESUS **IS** THE SON OF GOD. MAYBE--
WHEN PAUL'S OLD FRIENDS SEE HOW BOLDLY HE IS PREACHING ABOUT JESUS, THEY BECOME FURIOUS.
STOP HIM! STOP HIM BEFORE HE STIRS UP THE PEOPLE.
DEATH IS THE ONLY THING THAT WILL SILENCE A MAN LIKE PAUL.
THEN KILL HIM!

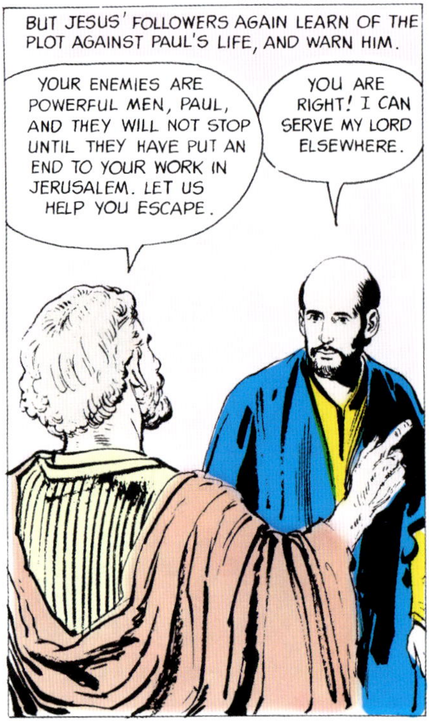

BUT JESUS' FOLLOWERS AGAIN LEARN OF THE PLOT AGAINST PAUL'S LIFE, AND WARN HIM.

YOUR ENEMIES ARE POWERFUL MEN, PAUL, AND THEY WILL NOT STOP UNTIL THEY HAVE PUT AN END TO YOUR WORK IN JERUSALEM. LET US HELP YOU ESCAPE.

YOU ARE RIGHT! I CAN SERVE MY LORD ELSEWHERE.

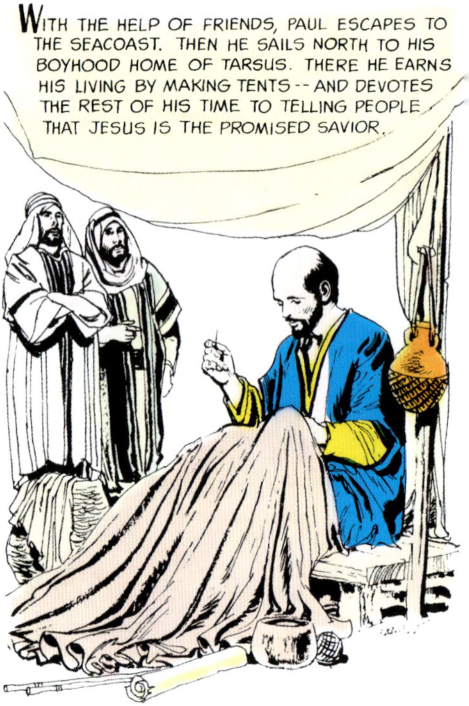

WITH THE HELP OF FRIENDS, PAUL ESCAPES TO THE SEACOAST. THEN HE SAILS NORTH TO HIS BOYHOOD HOME OF TARSUS. THERE HE EARNS HIS LIVING BY MAKING TENTS -- AND DEVOTES THE REST OF HIS TIME TO TELLING PEOPLE THAT JESUS IS THE PROMISED SAVIOR.

Foreign Assignment

From Acts 11:25-30; 12:25–13:7

After escaping from his enemies in Jerusalem, Paul returns to his boyhood home of Tarsus. For several years he works and preaches the gospel. One day an old friend comes to see him...

BARNABAS! WHAT BRINGS YOU TO TARSUS?

YOU, PAUL! I HAVE BEEN PREACHING IN ANTIOCH, AND THE CHURCH HAS GROWN SO MUCH THAT I NEED HELP. WILL YOU COME?

Eagerly Paul accepts the invitation.

THE CHURCH WAS STARTED BY PEOPLE WHO FLED FROM YOUR PERSECUTION IN JERUSALEM.

THANK GOD YOU ARE GIVING ME THE CHANCE TO ASK THEIR FORGIVENESS AND WORK WITH THEM IN SPREADING THE GOSPEL.

IN ANTIOCH, THE THIRD LARGEST CITY OF THE ROMAN EMPIRE, PAUL AND BARNABAS WIN BOTH JEWS AND GENTILES TO FAITH IN CHRIST. HERE THE FOLLOWERS OF JESUS ARE GIVEN THE NAME OF CHRISTIANS!

AFTER A TIME TEACHERS FROM JERUSALEM COME TO VISIT THE GROWING CHURCH ONE OF THEM, AGABUS, MAKES A TRAGIC PROPHECY.

I HAVE RECEIVED A WARNING FROM GOD THAT A GREAT FAMINE IS COMING. MANY OF OUR PEOPLE IN JERUSALEM ARE POOR. THEY WILL STARVE UNLESS--

PAUL INTERRUPTS EXCITEDLY.

LET US ALL GIVE WHAT MONEY WE CAN. I'LL HELP DELIVER IT!

BUT YOU HAVE ENEMIES IN JERUSALEM!

AND OUR LORD HAS FOLLOWERS THERE! WE MUST HELP THEM IN SPITE OF THE DANGER.

THE ANTIOCH CHRISTIANS GIVE GENEROUSLY, AND PAUL AND BARNABAS SET OUT FOR JERUSALEM WHERE THE FEAR OF HUNGER IS IN EVERY HOME.
WHAT WILL WE DO WHEN OUR FOOD IS GONE?
GOD WILL NOT FORSAKE US.
LISTEN-- SOMEONE'S AT THE DOOR.
BARNABAS!
PAUL AND I BRING HELP FROM THE CHRISTIANS IN ANTIOCH.
TAKE WORD TO THE OTHER ELDERS. WE MUST PURCHASE FOOD AND TAKE IT TO OTHERS AT ONCE.
TO THINK I EVER DOUBTED!

THEIR MISSION OVER, PAUL AND BARNABAS PREPARE TO LEAVE JERUSALEM.
PAUL, THIS IS MY COUSIN, MARK. HE WOULD LIKE TO GO WITH US.
GOOD! WE CAN USE YOU, MARK.

IN ANTIOCH THEY MEET WITH OTHERS FOR PRAYER. GOD TELLS THE LEADERS OF THE CHURCH THAT HE WANTS PAUL AND BARNABAS TO TAKE THE GOOD NEWS OF JESUS TO OTHER LANDS. THE TWO MEN ACCEPT THE CALL-- AND SET OUT WITH MARK.
THERE'S CYPRUS--- THE ISLAND WHERE I WAS BORN!
AND THAT'S WHERE OUR MISSIONARY WORK BEGINS.

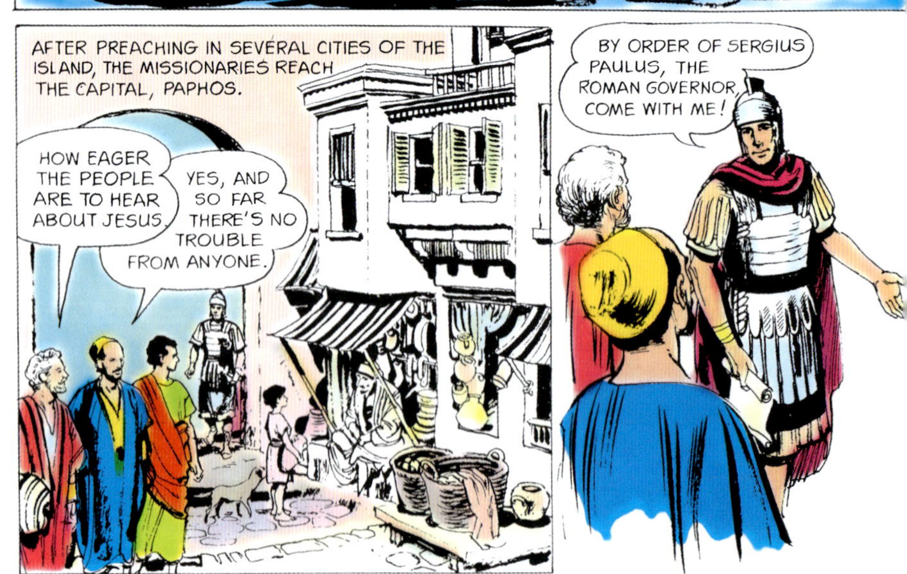
AFTER PREACHING IN SEVERAL CITIES OF THE ISLAND, THE MISSIONARIES REACH THE CAPITAL, PAPHOS.
HOW EAGER THE PEOPLE ARE TO HEAR ABOUT JESUS.
YES, AND SO FAR THERE'S NO TROUBLE FROM ANYONE.
BY ORDER OF SERGIUS PAULUS, THE ROMAN GOVERNOR, COME WITH ME!

The Enemy Strikes

From Acts 13:7-50

I CAN'T SEE! HELP ME--
SOMEBODY HELP ME!
ONLY GOD COULD DO THAT! ALL YOU HAVE TOLD ME ABOUT JESUS MUST BE TRUE. I BELIEVE IN HIM!
ENCOURAGED BY THEIR SUCCESS IN CYPRUS, THE MISSIONARIES GO ON TO ASIA MINOR. AT PERGA...
PAUL SAYS YOU'RE GOING NORTH TO ANTIOCH IN ASIA MINOR. THAT'S TOO FAR FROM HOME FOR ME! I'D LIKE TO GO BACK TO JERUSALEM.
I UNDERSTAND, MARK... GIVE OUR FRIENDS A REPORT OF THE WORK WE'RE DOING. AND ASK THEM TO PRAY FOR US.

Black Sea
ASIA MINOR
ANTIOCH
PERGA
TARSUS
ANTIOCH
SYRIA
CYPRUS
PAPHOS
Mediterranean Sea
DAMASCUS
CAESAREA
JERUSALEM
THE AREA IN WHICH PAUL AND BARNABAS TRAVELED.
ON THE ROAD TO ANTIOCH IN ASIA MINOR...
I'M DISAPPOINTED IN MARK.
HE'S YOUNG, PAUL, AND THIS WAS HIS FIRST EXPERIENCE IN FOREIGN COUNTRIES. HE'LL SERVE JESUS IN JERUSALEM -- AND THAT'S IMPORTANT, TOO.
IN ANTIOCH PAUL IS INVITED TO PREACH IN THE SYNAGOGUE. HIS SERMON ABOUT JESUS CAUSES SO MUCH EXCITEMENT THAT HE IS ASKED TO SPEAK AGAIN THE FOLLOWING WEEK. BUT NOT ALL WHO COME ARE PLEASED.
LOOK! THE CROWD IS LISTENING TO EVERY WORD HE SAYS. THIS MAN IS TRYING TO DESTROY US -- AND THE WHOLE JEWISH RELIGION.
I'LL PUT A STOP TO HIM -- RIGHT NOW!

THIS MAN IS A LIAR—AND A TRAITOR TO THE FAITH OF OUR FATHERS.

WE FELT IT OUR DUTY TO GIVE GOD'S MESSAGE OF EVERLASTING LIFE TO YOU JEWS FIRST, BUT IF YOU DO NOT WANT THE MESSAGE, WE'LL TAKE IT TO THE GENTILES!

THE GENTILES REACT WITH JOY AND THANKSGIVING.

THANK GOD FOR SENDING PAUL WITH SUCH GOOD NEWS!

ETERNAL LIFE WITH GOD—I MUST TELL MY FRIENDS AT ONCE!

BUT CERTAIN LOCAL JEWS ARE SO ANGRY THAT THEY CARRY THEIR CAMPAIGN OF LIES AGAINST PAUL TO THE LEADING CITIZENS OF ANTIOCH.

DON'T YOU SEE? PAUL IS TRYING TO CAUSE TROUBLE BETWEEN JEWS AND GENTILES. IF IT LEADS TO BLOODSHED THE GOVERNMENT IN ROME WILL SEND SOLDIERS TO INVESTIGATE--

WE KNOW HOW TO HANDLE TROUBLEMAKERS! PAUL AND HIS FRIEND MUST LEAVE AT ONCE --OR BE PUNISHED!

Paul, a Champion Who Switches Sides!

Paul is a great man of God who first kills Christians because he honestly believes they are going against God. Then when Jesus speaks to him directly on the road to Damascus, Paul realizes he has been on the wrong side. He becomes a great champion for the Gospel.

HERE ARE SOME OTHER INTERESTING FACTS ABOUT HIM:

- He has two names—Paul (Roman) and Saul (Hebrew) (Acts 13:9).
- He is a Jew and a Roman citizen (Acts 22:27).
- As a boy, he learns to make tents (Acts 18:3).
- At his conversion, he is blind for three days (p. 186).
- He writes 13 letters, called the Pauline Epistles, which become part of the Bible.

- Paul and Barnabas are the first Christian missionaries (p. 194).
- When Paul and Silas are thrown in jail for disturbing the peace, they sing praises to God, and God sends an earthquake to free them (p. 216).
- He faces danger and hardship as a missionary:
  5 times whipped
  3 times beaten with rods
  1 time stoned with rocks
  3 times shipwrecked
  plus bandits, hunger, thirst, cold
  (2 Corinthians 11:24-27).

But he later said:

> "I have kept the faith. Now there is in store for me a crown of righteousness" (2 Timothy 4:7–8).

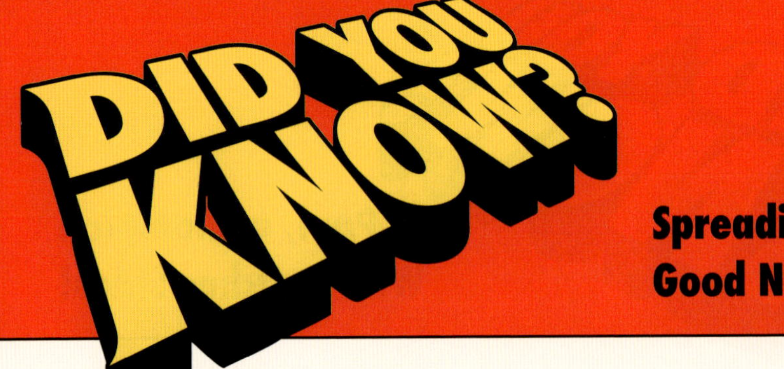

Spreading the Good News

Many people throughout history have chosen to follow Jesus' command to take the Gospel to all nations (see p. 136).

HERE ARE JUST A FEW:

- **William Carey** (1761-1834) went to India from England. Besides preaching the Gospel, Carey set up mission stations and schools, translated the Bible into several languages, and brought agricultural improvements to the Indian people.
- **Adoniram Judson** (1788-1850) was an American who went to Burma. After years of struggle and imprisonment, he translated the entire Bible into Burmese.
- **James Hudson Taylor** (1832-1905) was an English medical missionary to China. Unlike other missionaries, he dressed and ate like the Chinese people he served. Under his leadership, 800 missionaries served in the China Inland Mission from several church denominations.
- **Mary Slessor** (1848-1915) left Scotland to help the people of Nigeria, Africa. She taught the people to read the Bible and became a peacemaker among tribal chiefs. She wanted to reach tribes that had never heard of Jesus.
- **Amy Carmichael** (1867-1951) grew up in Northern Ireland, where she taught Sunday classes to mill workers. In 1895, she went to India. In addition to preaching the Gospel, she rescued many children from evil temple practices.

Miracle in Lystra

From Acts 13:51–14:19

THE MISSIONARIES ESCAPE AND HURRY ON TO THE CITY OF LYSTRA. ONE DAY AS PAUL IS PREACHING, HE NOTICES A LAME MAN LISTENING WITH KEEN INTEREST.
STAND UP ON YOUR FEET!
INSTANTLY THE MAN JUMPS UP.
I CAN WALK. GLORY TO GOD, I CAN WALK!
THESE STRANGERS ARE NOT ORDINARY MEN THEY ARE GODS WHO LOOK LIKE MEN!
THE PEOPLE SPEAK IN THE LANGUAGE OF LYSTRA, SO PAUL AND BARNABAS DO NOT UNDERSTAND HOW THE CROWD FEELS UNTIL THEY SEE A PRIEST BRINGING ANIMALS FOR SACRIFICE.
NO! NO! YOU MUST NOT WORSHIP US. WE ARE MEN, JUST LIKE YOU, BUT WITH A MESSAGE FROM THE ONE TRUE GOD. HE IS THE ONE WHO HEALED THE MAN!

BUT YOU ARE LIKE THE GODS JUPITER AND MERCURY.
JUPITER AND MERCURY ARE FALSE GODS. WORSHIP THE TRUE GOD WHO HAS SENT YOU RAIN FROM HEAVEN AND FRUIT IN ITS SEASON.
THE PEOPLE LISTEN EAGERLY. BUT, UNKNOWN TO PAUL AND BARNABAS, THEIR ENEMIES FROM ANTIOCH AND ICONIUM FOLLOW THEM TO LYSTRA. THEY SPREAD THEIR LIES AMONG THE SIMPLE PEOPLE.
PAUL AND BARNABAS CAUSE TROUBLE WHEREVER THEY GO. GET RID OF THEM AS WE DID!
THERE'LL BE NO TROUBLE IN LYSTRA. I'LL SEE TO THAT!
SO A MOB IS WHIPPED INTO ACTION!
THERE'S PAUL! STONE HIM!

Storm Warning

From Acts 14:19–15:1

WHIPPED INTO A RAGE BY MEN FROM ANTIOCH AND ICONIUM, THE PEOPLE OF LYSTRA TURN AGAINST PAUL AND STONE HIM.

WHEN THE STONING IS FINISHED, THE ANGRY MOB DRAGS PAUL'S BODY OUT OF THE CITY.

QUICKLY BARNABAS AND CHRISTIANS OF LYSTRA GATHER AROUND PAUL'S MOTIONLESS FORM. BUT AS THEY STAND WEEPING...
HE'S GETTING UP! THANK GOD, HE LIVES! HE LIVES!

PAUL! WE THOUGHT THEY HAD KILLED YOU!
THEY MEANT TO, BUT GOD HAS SAVED MY LIFE FOR A PURPOSE. COME, LET'S GO BACK INTO THE CITY.

BACK TO LYSTRA? THAT MOB WILL NEVER LET YOU OUT ALIVE!
GOD WILL PROTECT ME.

THE NEXT MORNING PAUL AND BARNABAS SET OUT FOR DERBE WHERE THEY WIN MANY FOLLOWERS TO JESUS. ONE DAY PAUL STATES THAT IT IS TIME TO START THEIR HOMEWARD JOURNEY.
I AGREE. THE SHORTEST ROUTE IS THROUGH THE MOUNTAINS BY THE WAY OF YOUR BOYHOOD HOME OF TARSUS.
NO-- WE MUST GO BACK THE WAY WE CAME. OUR CHRISTIAN FRIENDS MAY NEED OUR HELP.
SO, IN SPITE OF THE DANGERS, PAUL AND BARNABAS RETRACE THEIR STEPS, VISITING THE CITIES OF GALATIA AND ORGANIZING THE CHURCHES THEY STARTED BEFORE. AT LAST THEY SAIL TOWARD THEIR HOME BASE-- ANTIOCH IN SYRIA.
ON THEIR FIRST MISSIONARY JOURNEY TO THE GENTILES, PAUL AND BARNABAS TRAVELED SOME 1400 MILES BY LAND AND SEA, AND WERE GONE FROM HOME ABOUT TWO YEARS.
ANTIOCH
ICONIUM
LYSTRA
DERBE
Galatia
TARSUS
PERGA
ATTALIA
ANTIOCH
Syria
Mediterranean Sea
Cyprus
SALAMIS
PAPHOS
IN ANTIOCH THEY RECEIVE A ROYAL WELCOME. THE CHURCH IS PROUD OF ITS MISSIONARIES AND THANKFUL TO HAVE A PART IN HELPING OTHERS KNOW JESUS.
I AM GLAD SO MANY GENTILES HERE IN ANTIOCH HAVE BECOME CHRISTIANS.
YES, AND THEY ARE LOYAL, TOO!

WITH PAUL AND BARNABAS AS LEADERS, THE CHURCH IN ANTIOCH GROWS IN SIZE AND INFLUENCE. BUT ONE DAY A GROUP OF JEWISH CHRISTIANS FROM THE CHURCH IN JERUSALEM ARRIVES.
YOU GENTILES CANNOT BECOME CHRISTIANS UNLESS YOU FIRST PROMISE TO OBEY OUR JEWISH LAWS!
BY WHAT AUTHORITY DO YOU SAY THAT?
BY THE AUTHORITY OF JAMES, THE BROTHER OF JESUS, WHO IS NOW LEADER IN THE CHURCH IN JERUSALEM.
HOW CAN THIS BE TRUE? PAUL DOES NOT SAY SO. WHAT SHALL WE DO?
I DON'T KNOW. I'LL NEVER GIVE UP MY FAITH IN JESUS, BUT I CAN'T OBEY ALL THOSE JEWISH LAWS.
THEN YOU CANNOT BE A CHRISTIAN!
THE QUARREL GROWS-- JEWISH CHRISTIANS VERSUS GENTILE CHRISTIANS. THE CHURCH IN ANTIOCH IS IN DANGER OF SPLITTING IN TWO!

Council in Jerusalem

From Acts 15:1–13; Galatians

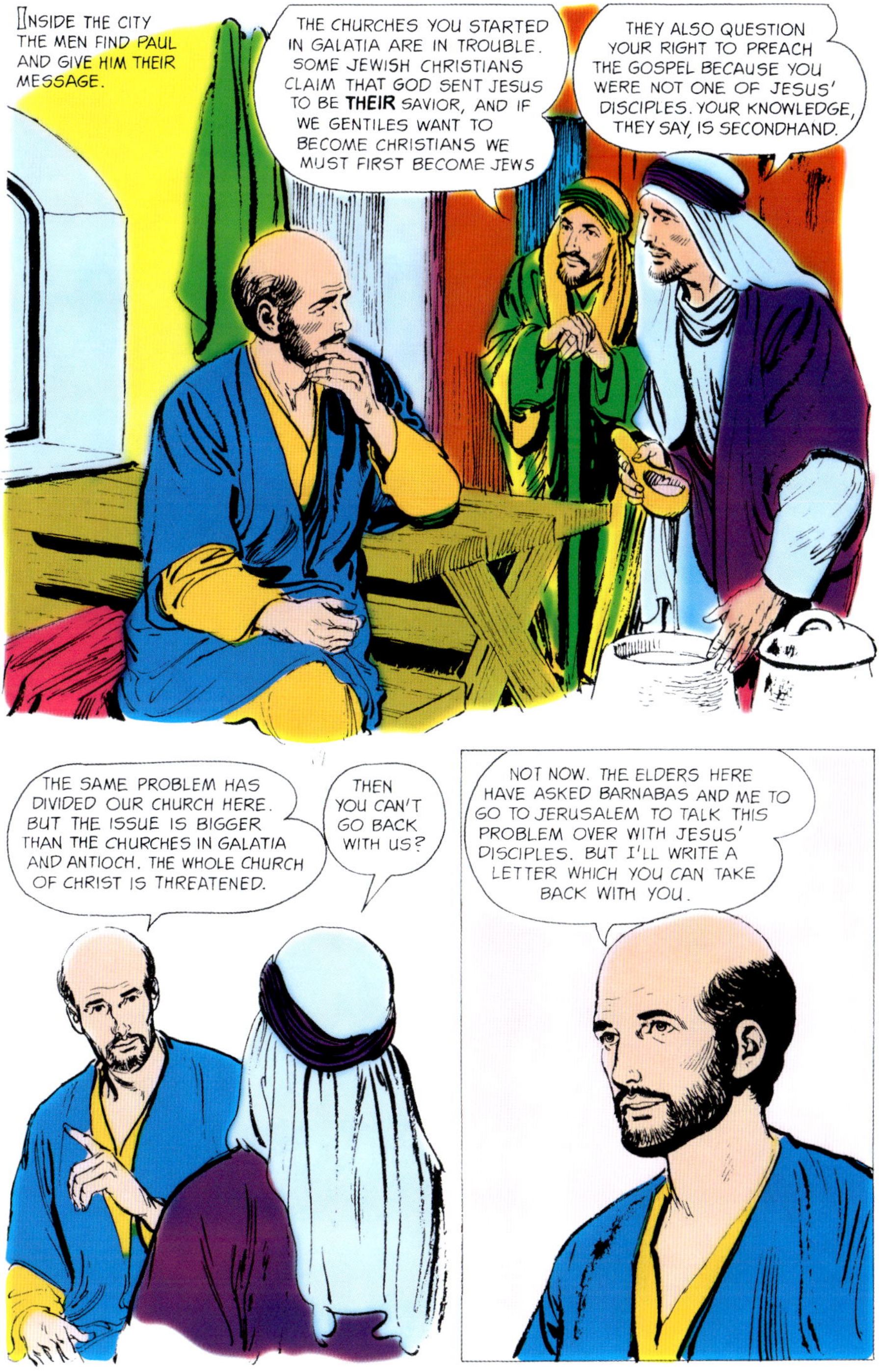

INSIDE THE CITY THE MEN FIND PAUL AND GIVE HIM THEIR MESSAGE.

THE CHURCHES YOU STARTED IN GALATIA ARE IN TROUBLE. SOME JEWISH CHRISTIANS CLAIM THAT GOD SENT JESUS TO BE **THEIR** SAVIOR, AND IF WE GENTILES WANT TO BECOME CHRISTIANS WE MUST FIRST BECOME JEWS

THEY ALSO QUESTION YOUR RIGHT TO PREACH THE GOSPEL BECAUSE YOU WERE NOT ONE OF JESUS' DISCIPLES. YOUR KNOWLEDGE, THEY SAY, IS SECONDHAND.

Second Journey

From Acts 15:13—16:8

THE NEWS IS RECEIVED WITH JOY IN ANTIOCH THAT JEWS AND GENTILES CAN GO ON WORKING TOGETHER FOR JESUS. WITH THIS SETTLED, PAUL IS FREE TO CONTINUE HIS MISSIONARY WORK IN GENTILE COUNTRIES.
BARNABAS, LET'S MAKE A TRIP TO VISIT THE CHURCHES WE STARTED.
GOOD IDEA-- I'D LIKE TO ASK MARK TO GO WITH US AGAIN.
NO--MARK LEFT US BEFORE.
I KNOW, BUT WE SHOULD GIVE HIM ANOTHER CHANCE.
PAUL DISAGREES. SO BARNABAS TAKES MARK AND SAILS TO THE ISLAND OF CYPRUS. PAUL TAKES SILAS WITH HIM BY LAND TO VISIT THE CHURCHES HE STARTED.
IN LYSTRA, THE CITY IN WHICH HE HAD BEEN STONED, PAUL FINDS A GROWING CHURCH.
PAUL, I WANT YOU TO MEET TIMOTHY. HE'S BECOME ONE OF OUR BEST YOUNG LEADERS.
I'VE HEARD MANY FINE REPORTS OF YOU, TIMOTHY. WOULD YOU LIKE TO GO WITH SILAS AND ME?

TIMOTHY EAGERLY ACCEPTS, AND THE CHURCH GIVES ITS BLESSING. SOON THE THREE TRAVELERS ARE ON THEIR WAY. GOD TELLS THEM NOT TO FOLLOW THE TRADE ROUTE TO EPHESUS, SO THEY GO NORTH AND WEST UNTIL THEY REACH TROAS ON THE AEGEAN SEA.

THERE GOOD FORTUNE AWAITS THE TRAVELERS.

DR. LUKE! THE LORD MUST HAVE LED YOU TO JOIN US HERE.

PAUL! I WILL TRAVEL WITH YOU.

AS THE FOUR MISSIONARIES WALK THROUGH THE STREETS OF THE GREAT SEAPORT...

ONE HUNDRED AND FIFTY MILES ACROSS THE SEA LIES MACEDONIA, THE LAND FROM WHICH ALEXANDER THE GREAT BEGAN HIS CONQUEST OF THE WORLD.

I WONDER WHERE GOD WANTS ME TO PREACH NEXT...

Call from across the Sea

From Acts 16:9-19

MACEDONIA
Black Sea
A GOOD WIND SPEEDS THE FOUR MISSIONARIES ACROSS THE AEGEAN SEA TO THE PORT OF NEAPOLIS. FROM THERE THEY WALK EIGHT MILES TO THE CITY OF PHILIPPI.
PHILIPPI
NEAPOLIS
THESSALONICA
SAMOTHRACE
TROAS
Aegean Sea
ASIA
ATHENS

THE CITY HAS NO SYNAGOGUE, SO ON THE SABBATH THEY WORSHIP BY A RIVERSIDE.
DO YOU HEAR THOSE WOMEN? THEY ARE PRAYING TO GOD.

THE MISSIONARIES JOIN THE WORSHIPERS--AND SOON PAUL IS TELLING THEM ABOUT JESUS. A LADY CLOTH MERCHANT, NAMED LYDIA, SPEAKS FIRST.
GOD HAS OPENED MY HEART TO BELIEVE IN HIS SON, JESUS. MAY I BE BAPTIZED?
OF COURSE, LYDIA.

SOON ALL OF THE MEMBERS OF LYDIA'S HOUSEHOLD ACCEPT JESUS AS THEIR SAVIOR. LYDIA INVITES THE MISSIONARIES TO MAKE HER HOME THEIR HEADQUARTERS WHILE IN PHILIPPI.

THE ROMANS LOVE PURPLE-- I SELL MOST OF MY CLOTH TO THEM.

AS YOU SELL TO THEM, TELL THEM ABOUT JESUS.

ONE DAY AS PAUL AND SILAS WALK THROUGH THE STREETS OF PHILIPPI...

THE POOR GIRL IS UNDER THE INFLUENCE OF AN EVIL SPIRIT. HER MASTERS ARE USING HER AS A FORTUNETELLER.

YOU ARE A MAN OF GOD!

IN CHRIST'S NAME, COME OUT!

LOOK! SHE CAN'T TELL FORTUNES ANY MORE. OUR BUSINESS IS RUINED. WHAT'LL WE DO?

WHOEVER THAT MAN IS, HE'LL PAY FOR MEDDLING IN OUR AFFAIRS. COME ON!

Earthquake

From Acts 16:20-37

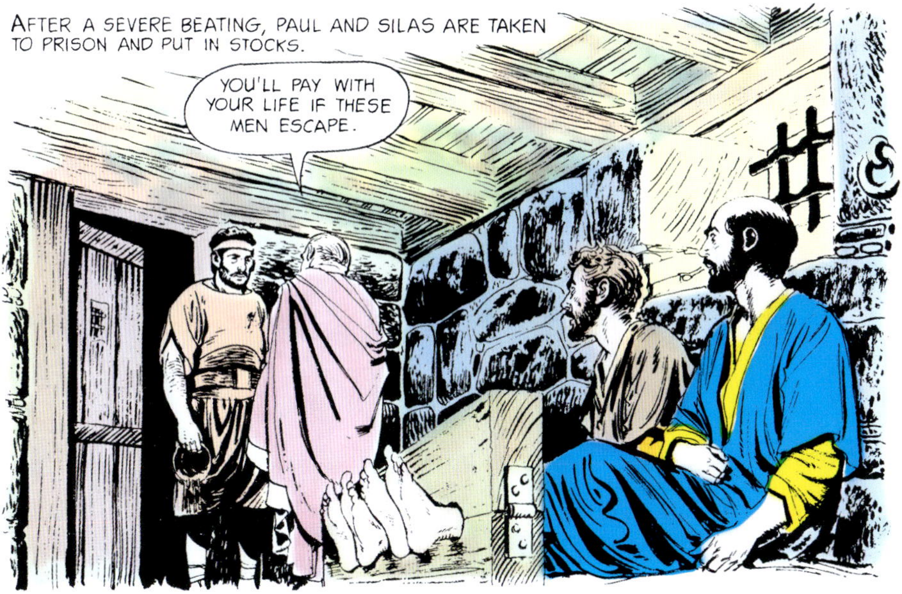

AFTER A SEVERE BEATING, PAUL AND SILAS ARE TAKEN TO PRISON AND PUT IN STOCKS.

YOU'LL PAY WITH YOUR LIFE IF THESE MEN ESCAPE.

BELIEVING THAT PAUL AND SILAS HAD SOMETHING TO DO WITH THE EARTHQUAKE THE JAILER FALLS ON HIS KNEES BEFORE THEM.

WHAT MUST I DO TO BE SAVED?

BELIEVE ON THE LORD JESUS CHRIST.

THE JAILER QUICKLY TAKES THE TWO PRISONERS TO HIS HOUSE AND TREATS THEIR WOUNDED BODIES. HE AND HIS FAMILY LISTEN EAGERLY AS PAUL TELLS THEM ABOUT JESUS -- AND ALL ARE BAPTIZED.

Out of Trouble ... into Trouble

From Acts 16:38–17:13

AT THE HOUSE OF LYDIA, PAUL, SILAS, AND TIMOTHY BID THEIR FRIENDS GOOD-BYE.

THANK YOU FOR LEAVING DR. LUKE HERE TO LEAD OUR CHURCH.
WE WILL RETURN SOMEDAY. HOLD FAST TO YOUR FAITH IN JESUS AND HELP OTHERS TO KNOW HIM.

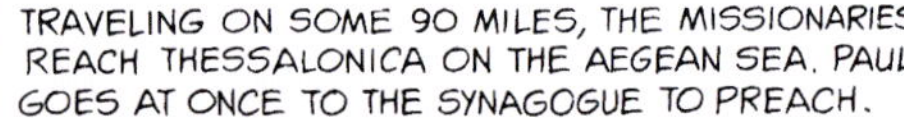
TRAVELING ON SOME 90 MILES, THE MISSIONARIES REACH THESSALONICA ON THE AEGEAN SEA. PAUL GOES AT ONCE TO THE SYNAGOGUE TO PREACH.

THE SCRIPTURES PROMISED THAT A SAVIOR WOULD COME. JESUS, WHO DIED ON THE CROSS AND ROSE FROM THE DEAD, IS THAT SAVIOR.

MANY PEOPLE LISTEN AND BELIEVE -- BUT SOME OF THE JEWISH LEADERS DO NOT.
HE'S STAYING AT JASON'S HOUSE. LET'S GET HIM THERE.
WE'VE GOT TO GET RID OF HIM BEFORE HE HAS THE WHOLE CITY BELIEVING WHAT HE SAYS.

GATHERING A STRONG-ARMED MOB, THE RELIGIOUS LEADERS CALL ON JASON.
IF YOU'RE LOOKING FOR PAUL, HE'S NOT HERE.
YOU'RE HIDING HIM. IF YOU WON'T LET US HAVE HIM, WE'LL TAKE YOU.

Paul Explains the "Unknown God"

From Acts 17:13–18:12; 1 and 2 Thessalonians

ON THE SABBATH PAUL PREACHES TO THE JEWS, BUT DURING THE WEEK HE CARRIES HIS MESSAGE OF JESUS TO THE GREEKS IN THE MARKET PLACE.
HE SAYS THERE IS ONLY ONE GOD, AND THAT HE SENT HIS ONLY SON, JESUS, TO SAVE US.
I'D LIKE TO HEAR MORE ABOUT A GOD WHO CARES FOR PEOPLE. LET'S ASK THIS MAN TO SPEAK BEFORE THE COURT OF MARS' HILL.
PAUL ACCEPTS THE INVITATION EAGERLY.
GENTLEMEN OF ATHENS, SINCE YOU WORSHIP A GOD YOU DO NOT KNOW, I'LL TELL YOU WHO HE IS--THE TRUE GOD, WHO MADE ALL THINGS. HE DOES NOT LIVE IN TEMPLES MADE BY HUMAN HANDS. HE IS NOT FAR FROM EACH ONE OF US, FOR IN HIM WE LIVE, AND MOVE, AND HAVE OUR BEING.
THE MEN OF ATHENS LISTEN EAGERLY--UNTIL PAUL SAYS THAT JESUS ROSE FROM THE DEAD.
NOBODY CAN BE RAISED FROM THE DEAD. WHAT A SILLY IDEA!
I'M NOT SO SURE...

AFTER PREACHING IN ATHENS WHERE A FEW BELIEVE, PAUL NEXT GOES TO CORINTH WHERE HE LOOKS FOR WORK.
MY NAME IS PAUL. I'M A TENTMAKER BY TRADE.
SO ARE WE. WHY DON'T YOU WORK WITH US? MY NAME IS AQUILA. THIS IS MY WIFE PRISCILLA.
I AM ALSO A MISSIONARY. MY REASON FOR COMING HERE IS TO START A CHRISTIAN CHURCH.
A CHURCH? THAT WON'T BE EASY. CORINTH IS A RICH CITY, BUT IT'S A WICKED ONE.
DURING THE WEEK PAUL EARNS HIS LIVING AS A TENTMAKER, AND ON THE SABBATH HE PREACHES IN THE SYNAGOGUE. ONE DAY...
SILAS! TIMOTHY! I'M SO GLAD THAT YOU HAVE COME!
TIMOTHY HAS BROUGHT A REPORT FROM THE CHURCH AT THESSALONICA.

PAUL'S **First Letter to the Thessalonians**, WHICH IS A BOOK OF THE NEW TESTAMENT.

To the church of the Thessalonians--from Paul, Silas, and Timothy

We remember how joyfully you turned from idols to serve the true God. Though we had to leave, it was good to receive news that you are standing true to your faith, even though people have been making it hard for you.

As we urged you when we were with you, live in the way that will please God, who invited you to have a place in His Kingdom. Keep on praying, and love one another more and more. I know you have worried about Christians who have died, but you need not. For Jesus promised that when He comes back from Heaven these will meet Him.

Be sure this letter is read to all the members of the church.

PAUL GETS FURTHER WORD FROM HIS FRIENDS IN THESSALONICA. HE WRITES A **Second Letter to the Thessalonians**. THIS ALSO IS A BOOK OF THE NEW TESTAMENT.

To the church of the Thessalonians--from Paul, Silas, and Timothy

Don't get a mistaken idea of what I told you. No one should quit working because he thinks Jesus will return right away. If anyone will not work, he should not be fed. Before Jesus comes, there will be a time when an evil man tries to rule the world, taking the place of God. But God will keep you from evil. Don't get discouraged in doing what is right.

In any letter that I send to you, I write a few words at the close in my own handwriting--like this--so that you will be sure the letter is from me. May Christ's love be with you all.

FOR A YEAR AND A HALF PAUL PREACHES IN CORINTH. A STRONG CHRISTIAN CHURCH IS STARTED. BUT THE JEWISH LEADERS ARE ANGRY AT PAUL AND LOOK UPON HIM AS A TRAITOR TO HIS RELIGION.

Talk of the Town

From Acts 18:13—19:16

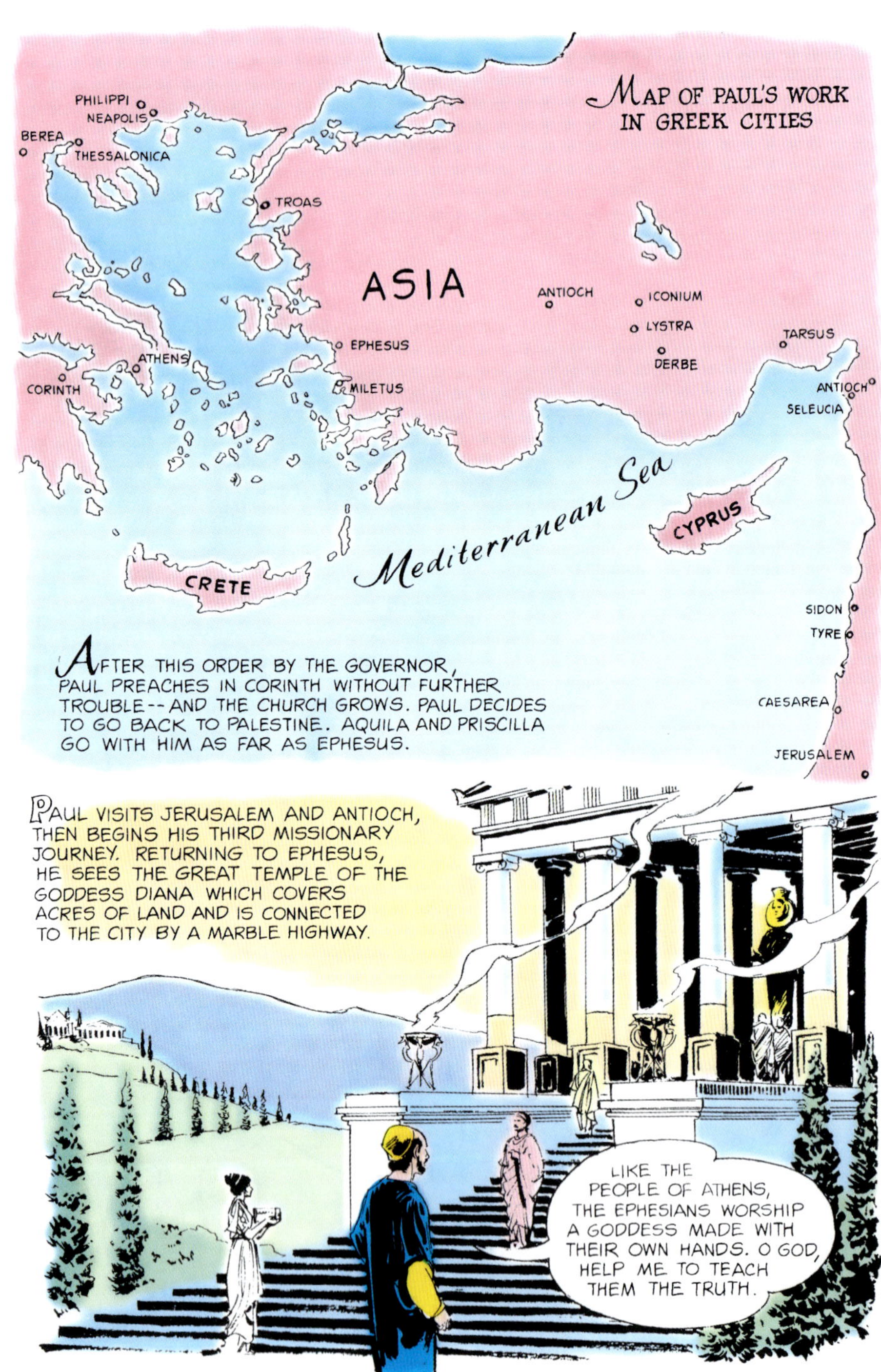
MAP OF PAUL'S WORK IN GREEK CITIES
PHILIPPI
NEAPOLIS
BEREA
THESSALONICA
TROAS
ASIA
ANTIOCH
ICONIUM
LYSTRA
DERBE
TARSUS
EPHESUS
ATHENS
CORINTH
MILETUS
ANTIOCH
SELEUCIA
Mediterranean Sea
CYPRUS
CRETE
SIDON
TYRE
CAESAREA
JERUSALEM
AFTER THIS ORDER BY THE GOVERNOR, PAUL PREACHES IN CORINTH WITHOUT FURTHER TROUBLE--AND THE CHURCH GROWS. PAUL DECIDES TO GO BACK TO PALESTINE. AQUILA AND PRISCILLA GO WITH HIM AS FAR AS EPHESUS.
PAUL VISITS JERUSALEM AND ANTIOCH, THEN BEGINS HIS THIRD MISSIONARY JOURNEY. RETURNING TO EPHESUS, HE SEES THE GREAT TEMPLE OF THE GODDESS DIANA WHICH COVERS ACRES OF LAND AND IS CONNECTED TO THE CITY BY A MARBLE HIGHWAY.
LIKE THE PEOPLE OF ATHENS, THE EPHESIANS WORSHIP A GODDESS MADE WITH THEIR OWN HANDS. O GOD, HELP ME TO TEACH THEM THE TRUTH.

The Angry Mob

From Acts 19:17–20; 1 Corinthians

PAUL IS STILL REJOICING WITH THE GROWTH OF THE CHURCH IN EPHESUS WHEN NEWS COMES FROM CORINTH...
THE CHURCH IN CORINTH IS HAVING ALL SORTS OF TROUBLES. THE MEMBERS ARE TAKING SIDES AGAINST ONE ANOTHER. SOME OF THEM SAY YOU ARE THE HEAD OF OUR CHURCH. OTHERS SAY APOLLOS IS THE BEST PREACHER--AND STILL OTHERS SAY PETER IS THE REAL LEADER CHOSEN BY JESUS.
PAUL DICTATES A LETTER TO THE CHURCH OF CORINTH, KNOWN AS I Corinthians, IT IS A BOOK OF THE NEW TESTAMENT.
Paul, to the church at Corinth...
I beg of you, my brothers, do not quarrel and divide the church. There is only one head of the Christian Church--Christ! It was Christ--not Paul or Apollos or Peter--who died for you on the cross.
Keep yourselves pure. Don't you see that you yourselves are the temple of God--and that God's Spirit lives in you? God will destroy anyone who defiles his temple, for his temple is holy--and that is what you are!
If I knew everything and could speak like an angel but did not have Christian love, I would amount to nothing. Be kind and love one another in the church. I send my love to all of you.
THE CHURCH IN EPHESUS GROWS-- ALMOST AS RAPIDLY AS THE BLAZE WHICH DESTROYED THE BOOKS OF MAGIC. IT HAS ITS EFFECT ON THE IDOL MERCHANTS OF THE CITY...
BUSINESS IS NO GOOD. PEOPLE AREN'T BUYING SILVER TEMPLES OF DIANA.
IT'S BECAUSE OF THAT CHRISTIAN PREACHER, PAUL. HE IS LEADING THE PEOPLE TO BELIEVE IN JESUS.

THE MERCHANTS COMPLAIN UNTIL THE HEAD OF THE SILVERSMITHS CALLS A MEETING.
PAUL TELLS PEOPLE DIANA IS NOT REALLY A GODDESS — THAT IT DOES NO GOOD TO WORSHIP HER.
EITHER PAUL GOES — OR WE'RE OUT OF BUSINESS!
WHIPPED INTO A FRENZY, THE SILVERSMITHS RUSH OUT INTO THE STREET.
WHERE'S PAUL? TELL US--
NEVER!

THE CROWD GROWS AS IT PUSHES THROUGH THE STREETS -- SOON THE WHOLE CITY IS IN AN UPROAR...
GREAT IS DIANA OF THE EPHESIANS!
AND THE MOB TAKES PAUL'S FRIENDS TO THE GREAT OUTDOOR THEATER.
A FEW MINUTES LATER IN ANOTHER PART OF THE CITY...
PAUL! THE SILVERSMITHS ARE AFTER YOU FOR DESTROYING THEIR BUSINESS. THEY HAVE SEIZED GAIUS AND ARISTARCHUS AND...
WHERE ARE THEY?
NO! PAUL! THAT MOB WILL KILL YOU!

Riot in Ephesus

From Acts 19:31–20:3; 2 Corinthians; Romans

IN FACE OF THIS THREAT, THE RIOT BREAKS UP. PAUL SENDS FOR HIS FRIENDS.

SOON AFTER PAUL REACHES PHILIPPI, TITUS JOINS HIM WITH NEWS FROM CORINTH.

PAUL, YOUR LETTER TO THE CHRISTIANS AT CORINTH MADE THEM CORRECT THEIR WRONG-DOING. BUT NOW SOME PEOPLE HAVE COME TO CORINTH WHO CLAIM YOU ARE NOT A TRUE APOSTLE OF JESUS.

ONCE AGAIN PAUL WRITES TO THE CHURCH IN CORINTH. THE LETTER--KNOWN AS II Corinthians--IS A BOOK OF THE NEW TESTAMENT.

I can see that my letter upset you, but I am glad I sent it. Not because I want to hurt you, but to make you sorry as God would have you sorry for the things that were wrong.

We are taking a collection for poor Christians in Jerusalem. Other churches have given large sums. I trust you will be able to do the same. Let everyone give what he has decided in his own heart to give, for God loves a cheerful giver.

And now, for those who question whether or not I am a true minister of Christ. I have been imprisoned, I have been beaten many times, I have often faced death. I have been stoned, I have been shipwrecked three times--all to carry out the work of Christ. When I visit you again, I hope it will be a happy meeting. Good-bye till then.

WHILE TITUS TAKES THE LETTER TO CORINTH, PAUL CONTINUES VISITING CHURCHES IN MACEDONIA, COLLECTING MONEY FOR THE POOR IN JERUSALEM. MONTHS LATER HE REACHES CORINTH WHERE HE IS GREETED BY FRIENDS WHO HAVE GIVEN EAGERLY TO HIS COLLECTION.

Bound Hand and Foot

From Acts 20:3—21:14

THE JEWISH BOAST FAILS. WARNED OF THE PLOT, PAUL MAKES A QUICK CHANGE OF PLANS AND TAKES THE LAND ROUTE NORTH TO MACEDONIA.
PAUL OUTWITTED HIS ENEMIES THIS TIME, BUT HOW LONG CAN HE ESCAPE THEIR HATE?
AFTER WEEKS OF TRAVEL AND VISITING CHURCHES ALONG THE WAY, PAUL REACHES TROAS. HE HAS SO MUCH TO TELL THE PEOPLE THAT HE TALKS FAR INTO THE NIGHT. OVERCOME BY SLEEP, A YOUNG MAN FALLS FROM AN UPPER WINDOW...
LOOK OUT!
HE FELL FROM THE THIRD STORY. HE MUST BE DEAD.
DON'T BE ALARMED. HE IS ALIVE.

THANK GOD!
HE WAS DEAD--I'M SURE HE WAS. WHAT POWER GOD HAS GIVEN PAUL!
AFTER PREACHING UNTIL DAYBREAK, PAUL SAYS GOOD-BY TO HIS FRIENDS.
MUST YOU GO, PAUL?
YES, I HAD PLANNED TO BE IN JERUSALEM FOR THE FEAST OF THE PASS-OVER, BUT I COULD NOT. NOW I WANT TO REACH THERE FOR THE FEAST OF PENTECOST.
AT MILETUS, PAUL SENDS WORD FOR THE ELDERS OF EPHESUS TO MEET HIM. EAGERLY THEY TRAVEL THE 35 MILES TO SEE HIM.
I MUST GO TO JERUSALEM--EVEN IF MY LIFE IS IN DANGER. I DO NOT CONSIDER MY LIFE IMPORTANT SO LONG AS I COMPLETE THE MINISTRY WHICH THE LORD GAVE ME. YOU ARE NOW SHEPHERDS OF THE CHURCH OF CHRIST--WHICH HE BOUGHT WITH HIS OWN LIFE. HELP THE WEAK--AND REMEMBER THE WORDS OF JESUS: TO GIVE IS BETTER THAN TO RECEIVE.

PAUL GOES ON TO TYRE, WHERE HE PREACHES FOR A WEEK. WHEN HE LEAVES, THE CHRISTIANS FOLLOW HIM TO THE BEACH FOR A PRAYERFUL GOOD-BY
DON'T GO TO JERUSALEM. SOME THERE ARE WAITING TO KILL YOU BECAUSE YOU SAY JESUS IS THE SON OF GOD.
I MUST GO. I HAVE MONEY WHICH GENTILE CHRISTIANS HAVE GIVEN ME FOR THE POOR IN JERUSALEM. I AM NOT AFRAID...
FARTHER DOWN THE COAST AT CAESAREA, PAUL VISITS WITH PHILIP THE EVANGELIST. THE PROPHET AGABUS JOINS THEM, AND--SUDDENLY-- WHILE THEY ARE TALKING HE TAKES PAUL'S BELT AND BEGINS TO BIND HIS OWN HANDS AND FEET.
WHAT DOES THIS MEAN?
THE HOLY SPIRIT TELLS ME THAT THE MAN TO WHOM THE BELT BELONGS WILL BE BOUND--LIKE THIS--BY SOME JEWS IN JERUSALEM AND HANDED OVER TO THE GENTILES.
PAUL-- GIVE UP YOUR PLANS TO GO TO JERUSALEM. FOR OUR SAKE--
WHY DO YOU TRY TO WEAKEN ME WITH YOUR TEARS? I AM PREPARED NOT ONLY TO BE BOUND, BUT TO DIE FOR THE SAKE OF THE LORD JESUS.

A Boy and a Secret

From Acts 21:15—23:24

IN ANGER THE PEOPLE TURN AGAINST PAUL. A MOB DRAGS HIM FROM THE TEMPLE AND STARTS TO BEAT HIM.
LOOK OUT-- ROMAN SOLDIERS ARE COMING!
NOW, TELL US WHAT THIS MAN HAS DONE.
TAKE HIM AWAY-- KILL HIM!
THE SOLDIERS CARRY PAUL TO THE PRISON. ON ITS STEPS PAUL STOPS AND TELLS THE PEOPLE HOW HE BECAME A CHRISTIAN, BUT WHEN HE MENTIONS PREACHING TO THE GENTILES, THE MOB GOES WILD.
HE IS NOT FIT TO LIVE!
KILL HIM!
KILL HIM!

Paul Pleads His Case

From Acts 23:25—28:4

FESTUS AND AGRIPPA WOULD HAVE SET PAUL FREE IF HE HAD NOT DEMANDED A TRIAL IN ROME. SO--UNDER ROMAN GUARD AND ACCOMPANIED BY LUKE--PAUL IS TAKEN ABOARD A SHIP BOUND FOR ROME. AT THE ISLAND OF CRETE...
THE WINTER STORMS WILL SOON BE HERE. IT WILL BE DANGEROUS TO GO ON UNTIL SPRING.
THE HARBOR AT PHOENIX IS NOT FAR AWAY--WE'LL SPEND THE WINTER THERE.
THE SHIP SETS SAIL--ONLY TO BE STRUCK BY A RAGING "NORTHEASTER."
TAKE DOWN THE MAINSAIL!
ON THE 14TH NIGHT OF THE STORM THE SAILORS TRY TO DESERT THE SHIP.
UNLESS THOSE MEN STAY WITH THE SHIP, YOU CANNOT BE SAVED!

THE SOLDIERS CUT THE SMALL BOAT LOOSE --AND THE SAILORS ARE FORCED TO STAY WITH THE SHIP. AT DAYBREAK...
LAND AHEAD!
HEADING TOWARD A BAY, THE SHIP RUNS AGROUND. THE BOW STICKS FAST, BUT THE STERN BEGINS TO BREAK UNDER THE POUNDING OF THE HEAVY WAVES.
ABANDON SHIP!
KILL THE PRISONERS--IF THEY REACH SHORE THEY'LL ESCAPE.
BECAUSE OF HIS FRIENDSHIP FOR PAUL, THE ROMAN OFFICER SPARES THE PRISONERS. SOLDIERS, SAILORS, PASSENGERS, AND PRISONERS STRUGGLE FOR THEIR LIVES IN THE RAGING SEA.

PAUL SHAKES OFF THE SNAKE INTO THE FIRE AND IS UNHARMED. THE PEOPLE WAIT FOR HIM TO BEGIN SWELLING OR SUDDENLY FALL DEAD, BUT AFTER THEY HAD WAITED A LONG TIME, THEY CHANGE THEIR MINDS AND BRING SICK PEOPLE TO HIM TO BE HEALED. THREE MONTHS LATER PAUL SAILS FOR ROME AND A LONG STAY IN PRISON.

Apostle on the March

From Philippians; 1 Timothy; Titus

As soon as he is well, Epaphroditus goes to see Paul.

THE CHURCH IN ROME IS GROWING RAPIDLY. UNLESS YOU NEED ME HERE, I WOULD LIKE TO GO BACK HOME.

YES, THAT'S WHAT YOU SHOULD DO. I HAVE WRITTEN A LETTER TO MY FRIENDS IN PHILIPPI. YOU CAN TAKE IT BACK WITH YOU.

Paul's letter to the *Philippians* is a book of the New Testament.

To the church at Philippi,

I don't know yet how my trial will come out, but I believe God will let me visit you again. Make me happy by living in harmony among yourselves. Think as Christ did. Though divine, He was willing to humble Himself and become a Man--willing even to die on the cross.

Thank you for your gift which Epaphroditus brought. You have been generous. God will also supply all that you need. Always be glad, since you are Christians, and think about the things that are good. The Christians here send greetings, especially the ones who are working in Caesar's palace.

Two years--and finally Paul's case is brought to court.* Before Nero, the most powerful ruler in the world, Paul makes his defense, and in a few days...

THANK GOD! NOW I CAN CARRY OUT MY DREAM TO TAKE THE GOSPEL OF CHRIST TO THE FARTHEST CORNERS OF THE EMPIRE!

*ALTHOUGH THE BIBLE DOES NOT TELL ABOUT PAUL'S RELEASE, THE LETTERS HE WROTE AFTERWARD SHOW THAT IT MUST HAVE TAKEN PLACE.

The Burning of Rome

From 2 Timothy; Hebrews 13:23

HISTORICAL BACKGROUND . . .

IT IS THE YEAR 64. NERO, THE CRUEL EMPEROR OF ROME, HAS MANY ENEMIES AMONG HIS OWN PEOPLE. THERE ARE RUMORS OF PLOTS AGAINST HIS LIFE. THEN, STRANGELY, A FIRE SWEEPS ACROSS THE CITY. FOR NINE DAYS IT RAGES--BURNING GREAT SECTIONS OF THE CITY AND DRIVING THOUSANDS FROM THEIR HOMES. FROM HIS PALACE, NERO WATCHES . . .

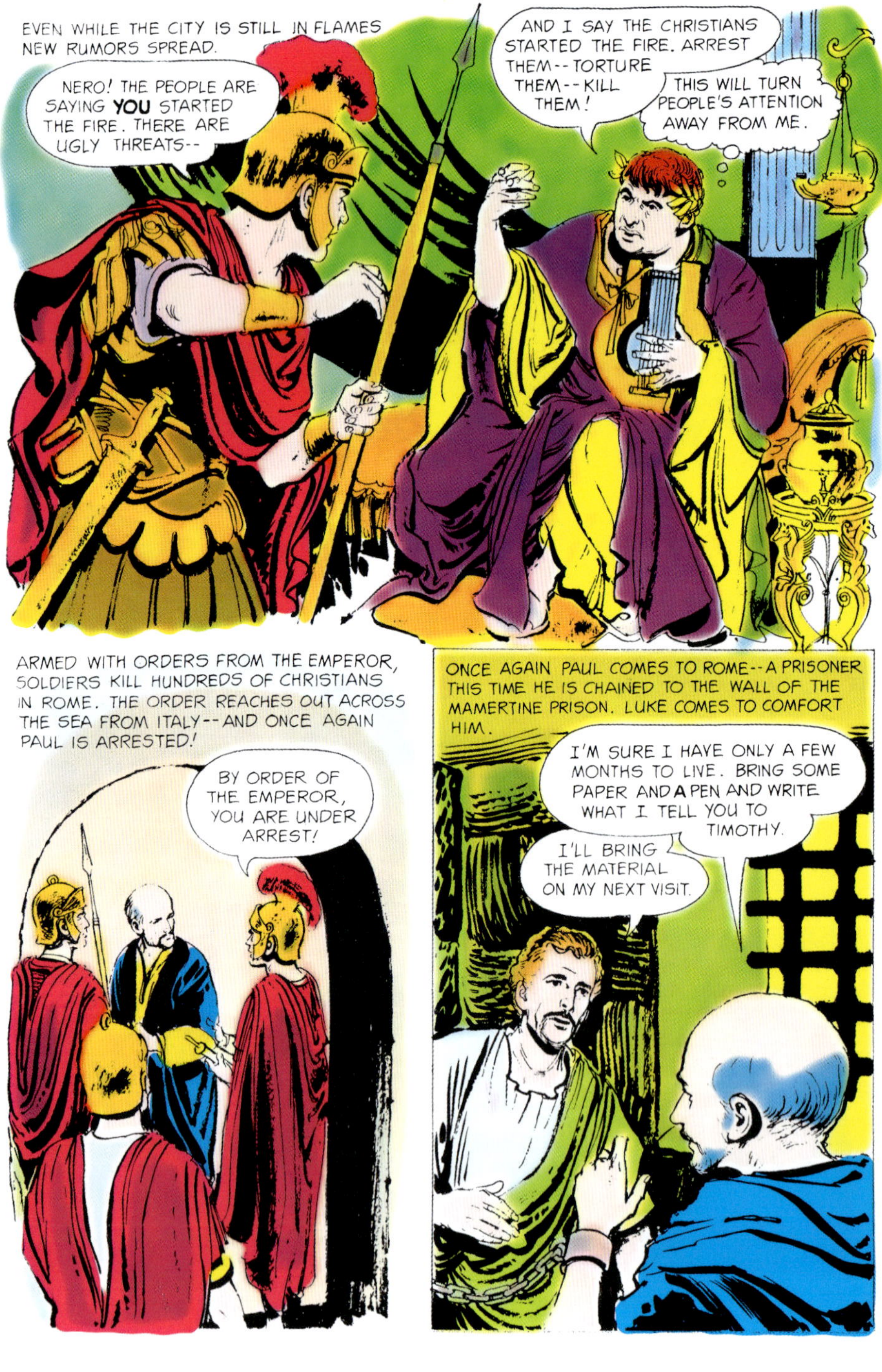

EVEN WHILE THE CITY IS STILL IN FLAMES NEW RUMORS SPREAD.

NERO! THE PEOPLE ARE SAYING **YOU** STARTED THE FIRE. THERE ARE UGLY THREATS--

AND I SAY THE CHRISTIANS STARTED THE FIRE. ARREST THEM--TORTURE THEM--KILL THEM!

THIS WILL TURN PEOPLE'S ATTENTION AWAY FROM ME.

ARMED WITH ORDERS FROM THE EMPEROR, SOLDIERS KILL HUNDREDS OF CHRISTIANS IN ROME. THE ORDER REACHES OUT ACROSS THE SEA FROM ITALY--AND ONCE AGAIN PAUL IS ARRESTED!

WHEN LUKE RETURNS, PAUL TELLS HIM WHAT TO WRITE. THE LETTER, **II Timothy**, IS A BOOK OF THE NEW TESTAMENT.

Dear Timothy,

Be strong, like a good soldier for Christ. Remember the truth as you learned from me and from the Holy Scriptures. Keep preaching it, even though the time will come when people don't want to hear the truth.

I want to see you very much. Do your best to come before winter. Bring the coat I left at Troas, and the books. I have almost reached the end of my life. Soon I will be with the Lord and He will give me a place in His heavenly Kingdom. Try to come soon.

Paul

WHEN TIMOTHY RECEIVES THE LETTER, HE SAILS AT ONCE TO ROME. THERE HE FINDS LUKE, WHO TAKES HIM TO THE PRISON. BUT AS TIMOTHY GREETS PAUL...

SO TIMOTHY, TOO, IS ARRESTED FOR TEACHING ABOUT JESUS. IN THEIR PRISON CELLS THE TWO MISSIONARIES WAIT FOR ROMAN LAW TO BRING THEM TO TRIAL. IN TIME PAUL'S CASE IS CALLED. ALONE, HE IS MARCHED TO THE COURT OF NERO.

Soldier Victorious

From 2 Timothy 4:6-8

QUICKLY SOLDIERS TAKE PAUL OUTSIDE THE CITY--TO BEHEAD HIM.
I HAVE FOUGHT THE GOOD FIGHT. I HAVE FINISHED MY COURSE. I HAVE KEPT THE FAITH.
SO DEATH COMES TO PAUL, WHO FOUNDED CHRISTIAN CHURCHES ON TWO CONTINENTS AND WHO WAS LED BY GOD TO WRITE NEARLY HALF OF THE BOOKS OF THE NEW TESTAMENT.
BUT PAUL'S DEATH DOES NOT BRING A HALT TO THE GOSPEL. CHRIST'S CHURCH MARCHES ON--THROUGHOUT THE ROMAN EMPIRE, AND THEN ACROSS THE WORLD.
Mediterranean Sea
EPHESUS
ASIA MINOR
Black Sea
EGYPT
CYPRUS
Nile R.
GAZA
JERUSALEM
DAMASCUS
MT. SINAI
Red Sea
Euphrates R.
Tigris R.

The End of an Era

Hebrews through Revelation

JESUS' DISCIPLES WHO WERE STILL ALIVE WERE GROWING OLD IN THE LATTER HALF OF THE FIRST CENTURY AFTER HIS BIRTH. THEY COULD NOT TRAVEL TO ALL THE CHURCHES, SO THEY TURNED TO WRITING LETTERS TO JESUS' FOLLOWERS.

THE LAST NINE BOOKS OF THE NEW TESTAMENT, HEBREWS THROUGH REVELATION, ARE MESSAGES THESE MEN WROTE TO GIVE ADVICE, COURAGE, AND COMFORT TO THE EARLY CHRISTIANS.

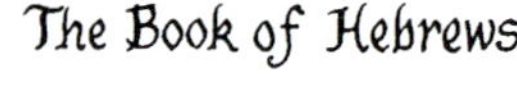

THE LETTER TO THE HEBREWS WAS WRITTEN AT A TIME WHEN JEWISH CHRISTIANS WERE BEING PRESSURED BY THE ROMANS AND JEWS TO GIVE UP THEIR FAITH IN JESUS.

THEY ASKED THEMSELVES: WHICH IS RIGHT, FAITH IN JESUS OR FAITH IN THE RELIGION OF OUR FOREFATHERS ABRAHAM, MOSES, AND DAVID?

"GOD HAS SPOKEN TO US THROUGH HIS SON, JESUS," THE LETTER SAID. "ABRAHAM, MOSES, AND DAVID WERE GREAT MEN WHO LIVED BY FAITH. THEY DIED; BUT JESUS CHRIST WILL LIVE FOREVER. HOLD FAST TO YOUR FAITH IN HIM."

THE LETTER ALSO BROUGHT THE GOOD NEWS THAT TIMOTHY HAD BEEN RELEASED FROM PRISON.

The Book of James

AS LEADER OF THE CHURCH IN JERUSALEM, JAMES, THE BROTHER OF JESUS, WROTE A LETTER OF ADVICE TO CHRISTIANS LIVING IN OTHER COUNTRIES.

"True religion is shown by what you do. Help those who need help. Be fair to all people. Ask God for wisdom, and keep your lives pure."

THUS THE BROTHER OF JESUS, WHO WAS KNOWN AS JAMES THE JUST, CONTINUED TO SPREAD THE GOSPEL.

The Book of II Peter

PETER KNEW THAT HE DID NOT HAVE MANY YEARS TO LIVE. HE WANTED TO HELP THE FOLLOWERS OF JESUS TO BE TRUE TO HIM, SO HE SENT THEM THIS LETTER.

"You believe in Jesus," he wrote. "Then act the way His followers should." Then he warned the Christians not to be upset by people who laughed at them because they believed that Jesus would return.

"When the time is right," Peter wrote, "Christ will return.

"God is giving people a chance to repent. He has promised a new world for those who love and obey Him.

"See how important it is for you to live for God!"

THESE ARE THE LAST WORDS WE HEAR FROM THE FISHERMAN WHO GAVE UP HIS NETS TO FOLLOW JESUS.

The Book of I John

JOHN, WHO HAD BEEN SO CLOSE TO JESUS IN EARLIER YEARS, WAS NOW THE LEADER OF THE CHRISTIANS AROUND EPHESUS.

"I have been with Jesus," John wrote to his people, "and I want you to have the same joy in knowing Him that I have. Don't believe anyone who says that God's Son did not come to the world as a real Person. God loved us and sent His Son to be our Savior. As He loved us, we should love one another."

The Book of II John

"I was very glad," John wrote, "to find some of your children living by the truth and obeying God's command to love one another. If any enemies of the truth come to you teaching that Christ was not a real man, do not receive them into your house. If you do, you will be helping in this evil work."

The Book of III John

"Dear Gaius," John wrote to his Christian friend, "I have heard good things about you. You are doing right in receiving Christians into your home, especially traveling preachers. Your kindness helps in their work. Don't pay attention to anyone who tries to stop you from doing this."

The Book of Jude

JUDE, ANOTHER BROTHER OF JESUS, DID NOT BELIEVE THAT JESUS WAS THE SON OF GOD--UNTIL HE ROSE FROM THE DEAD. THEN JUDE BECAME A CHRISTIAN AND AFTER THAT HE WAS A STRONG WORKER FOR CHRIST.

ONE DAY HE RECEIVED BAD NEWS--THAT PEOPLE IN SOME OF THE CHURCHES WERE TEACHING THINGS THAT WERE NOT TRUE.

JUDE WROTE THE CHURCHES A LETTER:

"You must defend our Christian faith. You have been warned that people would try to turn you away from Christ. I understand some of these false teachers are with you now. Pray that God will keep you strong, and that He will help you strengthen others."

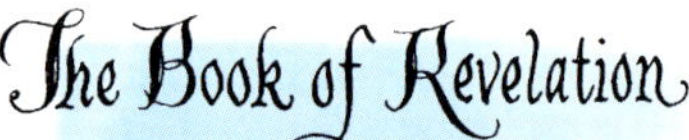

JOHN, WHO WROTE THE BEST-LOVED GOSPEL AND THREE LETTERS TO THE FOLLOWERS OF JESUS, ALSO WROTE THE BOOK OF REVELATION--TO HELP CHRISTIANS FACE THE ANGRY POWER OF ROME.

THE ROMANS HAD ARRESTED JOHN AND SENT HIM AS A PRISONER TO THE ISLAND OF PATMOS. THERE HE SAW A VISION OF HEAVEN, AND HE HEARD JESUS SAY:

"BEHOLD, I STAND AT THE DOOR, AND KNOCK: IF ANYONE HEARS MY VOICE, AND OPENS THE DOOR, I WILL COME INSIDE."

IN HEAVEN, JOHN SAW THE BOOK OF LIFE--IN WHICH WERE WRITTEN THE NAMES OF THOSE WHO LOVE CHRIST. AND FINALLY, THE OLD DISCIPLE SAW THE HOLY CITY, WHERE THERE IS NO SICKNESS, NO SORROW, NO DEATH. THOSE WHOSE NAMES ARE IN THE BOOK OF LIFE WILL ENTER THE GLORIOUS CITY AND LIVE FOREVER WITH CHRIST!

AND WITH JOHN'S VISION ENDS THE GREATEST STORY EVER TOLD, THE STORY OF THE BIBLE.

Life
in
Bible
Times

Life in Bible Times

IT'S EASY TO TAKE SOME OF OUR MODERN-DAY CONVENIENCES FOR GRANTED, ISN'T IT? HAVE YOU EVER WONDERED WHAT IT WOULD HAVE BEEN LIKE TO LIVE WHEN JESUS DID? IF YOU WANTED A DRINK, A TRIP TO THE LOCAL WELL WAS IN ORDER.

IN THIS SECTION, YOU'LL SEE WHAT LIFE WAS LIKE TWO THOUSAND YEARS AGO IN PALESTINE.

WHEN IT'S TIME FOR BED AND THE FIRE HAS DIED DOWN TO A FEW GLOWING COALS, A BOARD WILL BE LAID OVER IT AND THEN A CARPET. THIS KEEPS THE ROOM WARM FOR HOURS. THE FAMILY SLEEPS ON MATTRESSES SPREAD ON THE FLOOR.

AT HOME IN PALESTINE

THE LOWER FLOOR OF THE AVERAGE HOUSE WAS USED AS A STABLE FOR ANIMALS WHEN THEY COULDN'T BE LEFT OUTDOORS. AT OTHER TIMES IT SERVED AS A WORKSHOP OR A PLAYROOM.

OST HOMES IN PALESTINE
D TWO FLOORS. THE PEOPLE
SED THEIR FLAT ROOFS
R MANY ACTIVITIES, BUT
HE SECOND FLOOR WAS
IR MAIN LIVING QUARTERS.
HERE THEY SLEPT AT
GHT, DID THEIR COOKING
STORED THEIR BELONGINGS.
IS PICTURE WE SEE A TYPICAL
FAMILY IN THE SECOND
FLOOR OF THEIR HOME.
ATHER IS BRINGING HOME
SACK OF WHEAT. THE GIRL
BOY ARE GRINDING FLOUR.
HER IS TAKING SOMETHING
OUT OF ONE OF THE
SETS" (THEIR CLOSETS WERE
ST "PIGEON HOLES" IN THE
D WALLS). THE FIRE IS
ARGE HOLE IN THE FLOOR,
FILLED WITH BURNING
CHARCOAL.
ONE THING TO BE SAID IN FAVOR OF THE CLOTHING STYLES IN JESUS' TIME IS THAT THEY DIDN'T CHANGE FROM YEAR TO YEAR AS OURS DO TODAY. SOME PEOPLE LIVING IN THAT PART OF THE WORLD TODAY DRESS ALMOST THE SAME AS THEY DID IN BIBLE TIMES.
"FAMILY FASHIONS in the FIRST CENTURY"
LABORERS USUALLY WORE ONLY THE UNDERGARMENT—WITH OR WITHOUT SLEEVES—OR MERELY A WAIST-CLOTH WHICH REACHED TO THEIR KNEES.
A WIDE GIRDLE AROUND THEIR WAIST SERVED AS "POCKETS" IN WHICH THEY CARRIED MONEY, FOOD, A SWORD OR DAGGER, ETC.
SOME WORE A PLAIN SHEET WOUND AROUND THE BODY WITH ONE END FLUNG OVER THE SHOULDER. JESUS IS USUALLY PICTURED DRESSED THAT WAY.
GIRLS WORE THE SAME KIND OF CLOTHING AS THEIR MOTHERS WORE... WHICH, BY THE WAY, WAS PRACTICALLY THE SAME AS THE MEN WORE. IN FACT, SOME OF THE GARMENTS WERE SO MUCH ALIKE THAT THEY COULD BE WORN BY EITHER MEN OR WOMEN, AND NO ONE WOULD KNOW THE DIFFERENCE, EXCEPT FOR THE HEADDRESS. WOMEN AND GIRLS WORE LONG HEAD SCARFS.

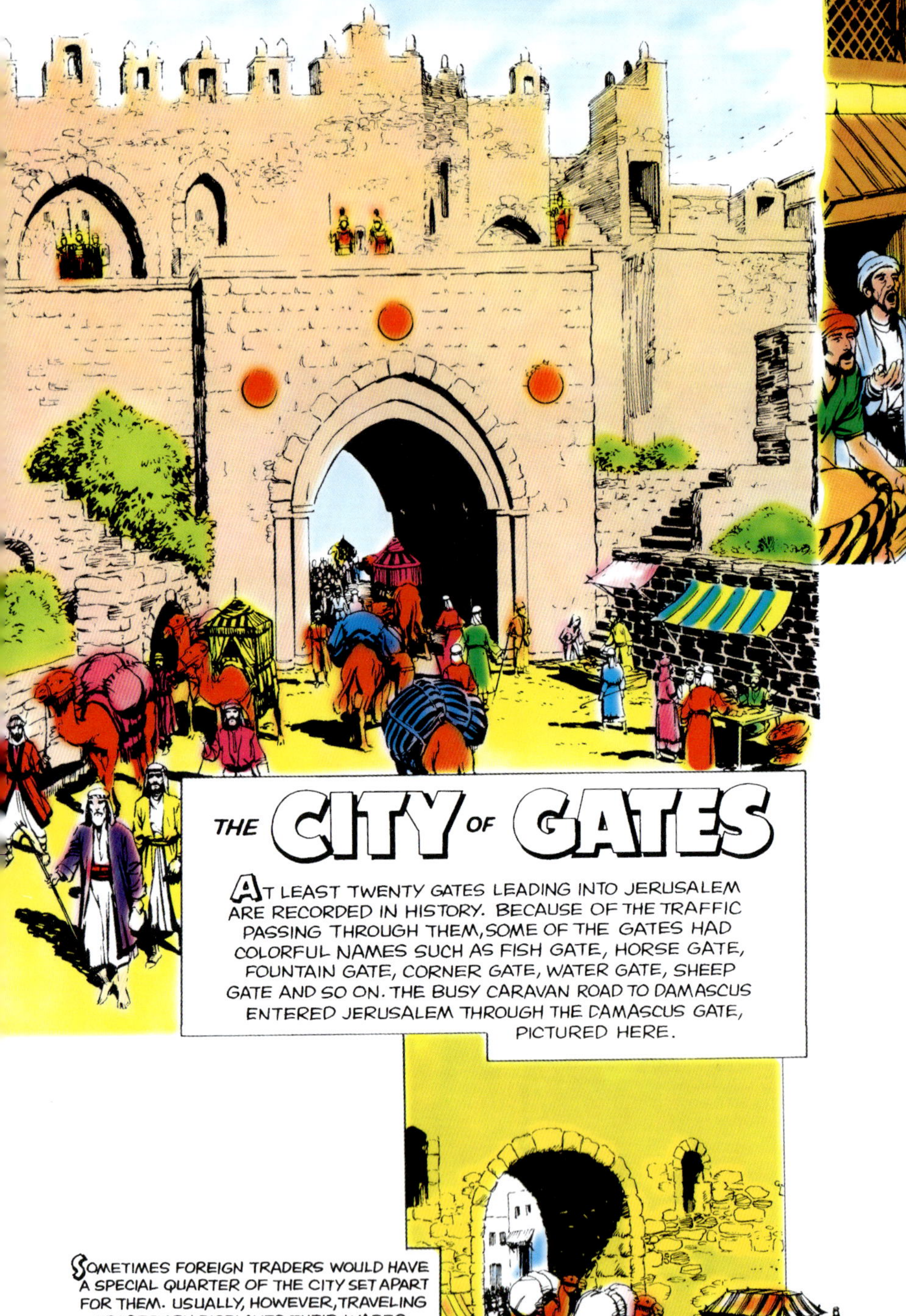
THE CITY OF GATES
AT LEAST TWENTY GATES LEADING INTO JERUSALEM ARE RECORDED IN HISTORY. BECAUSE OF THE TRAFFIC PASSING THROUGH THEM, SOME OF THE GATES HAD COLORFUL NAMES SUCH AS FISH GATE, HORSE GATE, FOUNTAIN GATE, CORNER GATE, WATER GATE, SHEEP GATE AND SO ON. THE BUSY CARAVAN ROAD TO DAMASCUS ENTERED JERUSALEM THROUGH THE DAMASCUS GATE, PICTURED HERE.
SOMETIMES FOREIGN TRADERS WOULD HAVE A SPECIAL QUARTER OF THE CITY SET APART FOR THEM. USUALLY, HOWEVER, TRAVELING TRADESMEN DISPLAYED THEIR WARES BOTH IN AND OUTSIDE OF THE CITY'S GATES.

A SHEKEL COINED ABOUT 140 B.C.

OCCUPATIONS IN BIBLE TIMES

FARMERS IN JESUS' TIME DIDN'T LIVE ON THEIR FARMS. THEY LIVED IN THE VILLAGES FOR MUTUAL PROTECTION FROM WILD ANIMALS AND BANDITS. EACH MORNING THE FARMERS WOULD DRIVE THEIR ANIMALS TO THEIR FIELDS FOR THE DAY'S WORK, WHICH BEGAN AT SUNRISE AND ENDED AT SUNSET.

MOST OF THE SMALL FARMS IN PALESTINE WERE WORKED BY THE FARMER'S FAMILY. BUT MANY MEN WHO DID NOT OWN FARMS WOULD HIRE THEMSELVES OUT AS FARM WORKERS.

A SHEPHERD'S LIFE IN BIBLE TIMES WAS FILLED WITH DANGER AND HARDSHIP. HE WAS ON GUARD DAY AND NIGHT PROTECTING HIS SHEEP FROM RUSTLERS AND WILD ANIMALS. HIS DEFENSES AGAINST THESE LURKING DANGERS WERE HIS STAFF, HIS SLING AND HIS COURAGE.

SHEPHERDS USED A SLING WITH AMAZING ACCURACY. THE SMALL STONES THEY HURLED STRUCK WITH TERRIFIC FORCE. DAVID SLEW THE GIANT GOLIATH WITH A SHEPHERD'S SLING. (I SAMUEL 17:32–51)
THE SLING WAS A SHORT STRIP OF LEATHER. A WIDE PIECE IN THE CENTER HELD THE SMALL STONE. AFTER WHIRLING THE SLING AROUND HIS HEAD A FEW TIMES, THE SHEPHERD LET GO OF ONE END, SENDING THE STONE SPEEDING LIKE A BULLET TOWARD THE TARGET.
AT NIGHT FLOCKS WERE BROUGHT INTO A SHEEPFOLD FOR PROTECTION. AS EACH SHEEP ENTERED, IT WAS COUNTED–EVEN CALLED BY NAME. THROUGHOUT THE NIGHT THE SHEPHERD SLEPT AT THE OPENING OF THE FOLD, ACTING AS THE VERY GATE ITSELF.
LIFE IN BIBLE TIMES WAS QUITE DIFFERENT FROM TODAY. BUT THE WORDS JESUS PREACHED IN THE NEW TESTAMENT APPLY TO US AS MUCH AS THEY DID TO THESE PEOPLE WHO LIVED 2,000 YEARS AGO.

Scripture Index

~M~

~P~

~R~

~T~